Al Ghazali
on
Islamic
Guidance

Muhammad Abul Quasem

Dar Ul Thaqafah

Dar ul Thaqafah

www.darulthaqafah.com

https://twitter.com/darulthaqafah

Email: darulthaqafah@gmail.com

Find our titles on your favorite online bookstore using the keyword 'Dar Ul Thaqafah'.

2023 CE – 1444 H

Translation of the Qur'ān

It should be perfectly clear that the Qur'ān is only authentic in its original language, Arabic. Since perfect translation of the Qur'ān is impossible, we have used the translation of the meaning of the Qur'ān throughout the book, as the result is only a crude meaning of the Arabic text.

Qur'ānic verses appear in speech marks proceeded by a reference to the Surah and verse number. Sayings (*Hadith*) of Prophet Muhammad (saw) appear in inverted commas along with reference to the Hadith Book and its Reporter.

AL-GHAZĀLĪ ON ISLAMIC GUIDANCE

CONTENTS

GENERAL INTRODUCTION

قل: ياايها الناس قد جاءكم الحق من ربكم؛ فمن اهتدى
فانما يهتدى لنفسه ومن ضل فانما يضل عليها. ـ قرآن ١٠:١٠٨

Say: O you people, the truth has indeed come from your Lord. Then whosoever follows the guidance, follows it only for the good of his own self and whosoever errs does so only to his own detriment. — Qur'ān: 10:108

والذين اهتدوا زادهم هدى واتاهم تقواهم. ـ قرآن ١٧ : ٤٧

God gives increased guidance to those who follow (His) guidance, and bestows righteousness upon them. — Qur'ān 47:17

The prime man, Adam, when descending from heaven to this world of water and clay, was told by God that he would be provided with guidance and that whoever would follow it would be happy in this life as well as in the Hereafter.[1] Adam eventually received divine guidance and so did his children in different ages in the form of revelations sent to numerous prophets and messengers of God. The final guidance designed by God for all human beings from the advent of Islam to Doomsday is, according to Islamic teaching,[2] contained in the Qur'ān revealed to the prophet Muḥammad (may peace be upon him!). The Prophet led his life fully following this guidance[3] and explained its various aspects through his words and deeds which all are recorded in the authentic works on Tradition (*ḥadīth*). His companions imitated him and felt no need to formulate any theory of guidance in the light of the Qur'ān and his words and deeds. However, such a need arose in the time of their followers for reasons which need not be mentioned here. From that time until about 950 A.D. — a period called the formative period of Islamic thought — several types of theories of guidance were formulated by different classes of Muslim intellectuals, such as jurists, theologians,

---

[1] Qur'ān 2:38.   [2] Qur'ān 34:28, 7:158.

[3] Muslim, *Ṣaḥīḥ*, Musāfirīn, 139; Abū Dāwūd, *Sunan*, Taṭawwu', 26; Ibn Ḥanbal, *Musnad*, VI, 54, 91, 188, 216.

ascetics, ṣūfīs, and philosophers.

In the eleventh century A.D. there was a great deterioration in Muslims' belief and observance of the Sharī'a as a result of the evil influence of al-Fārābī and Ibn Sīna's Neoplatonic philosophy, of Shī'a Bāṭinism, of false ṣūfīs and of evil religious scholars.[4] It was at this time of laxity in beliefs and practices that Abū Ḥāmid Muḥammad al-Ghazālī (d. 505/1111) flourished as a renewer (*mujaddid*)[5] of the religion of Islam and as one of the greatest intellectuals of Islamic history.[6] Well versed in almost all major intellectual disciplines of the time, al-Ghazālī refuted the prevailing false beliefs completely and fully exposed the wrongness of existing practices. As substitutes to these, he presented a belief system following the Ash'arite sunnī tradition and a system of practices in the light of the Qur'ān and Tradition, jurisprudence, ṣūfīsm, and his own thoughts and experiences. This system of practices may be called al-Ghazālī's theory of Islamic guidance, an aspect of which is set forth in the present work.

In this aspect of his theory al-Ghazālī first insists on the following of guidance, maintaining that it is the receipt of guidance, and not any worldly gain or mere information, which is the correct aim of acquisition of Islamic religious knowledge. Guidance has a beginning and an end, an outward aspect and an inward; the end can be reached only after the completion of the beginning. Al-Ghazālī makes it clear that his aim in this book is only to treat the beginning of guidance, and that anyone desirous of seeking knowledge of the end of guidance before completing the practice of its beginning is misled by Satan. In this connection al-Ghazālī points out three aims of seeking religious knowledge, two of which are condemned by him as wrong.

Al-Ghazālī defines the beginning of guidance as outward piety and the end of guidance as inward piety — only through piety can good consequences be achieved and only the pious are rightly

---

[4] Abū Ḥāmid Muḥammad al-Ghazālī, *al-Munqidh min aḍ-Ḍalāl*, Eng. trans. by W. Montgomery Watt, London, 1953, pp. 71-74.

[5] There is a Tradition that the Prophet said that at the beginning of every century God will send someone to revive and revitalize the faith of the Islamic community (Abū Dāwūd, *Sunan*, Cairo: al-Maktaba at-Tijāriyya, 1935, II, 424). Al-Ghazālī is generally considered to be the reviver of the fifth century of the Islamic era. He himself was convinced that he was the man chosen by God for this purpose. See his *Munqidh*, p. 75.

[6] Al-Ghazālī is even acclaimed by many, both in the East and the West, as the greatest religious authority of Islam after the Prophet.

guided. He defines piety as carrying out the commands of God and His messenger Muḥammad and turning aside from all that they have prohibited. Thus the beginning of guidance or outward piety consists in obedience to those commands and prohibitions of God and His messenger which are related to man's outward aspect or the body, while the end of guidance or inward piety lies in obedience to those commands and prohibitions which concern man's inward aspect or the soul. To be more precise, inward piety means purification of the soul from vices or evil qualities,[7] while outward piety or the beginning of guidance means performance of good acts of the body and avoidance of sins committed by it. Good acts of the body are subsumed under two heads: acts of obedience to God and good manners of companionship with one's fellow men. Thus the beginning of guidance or outward piety concerns (1) acts of obedience to God, (2) sins committed by the body, and (3) good manners of association with people. Al-Ghazālī discusses these three parts one after another, and the main points of his discussion may be mentioned here so that the reader may find it easy to follow it.

The beginning of guidance or piety in the acts of obedience to God is in force from the time of a man's waking up from sleep at dawn until the time of his return to bed at night. Al-Ghazālī gives a detailed account of this by stating what a man practising guidance is required to do when waking up from sleep at dawn, when going to and coming from the lavatory, when getting ritually clean whether through ablution or through bathing, when performing the Dawn Prayer, then in the time before sun-rise, then in the hours between the sun-rise and the Noon Prayer, between the Noon Prayer and the Lateafternoon Prayer, between the Lateafternoon Prayer and the Sunset Prayer, between the Sunset Prayer and the Evening Prayer, and finally between the Evening Prayer and preparing for sleep. Al-Ghazālī states the requirements of outward piety in each of these ritual prayers and in one's proceeding towards the mosque, entering it, staying inside it even though for a little while, and coming out of it. The excellence of the time before sun-rise and sunset is stressed, and the devotional acts by which this time can be utilized in the best way are mentioned. Four alternative excellent ways of passing the major part of the day are discussed in gradation of merit, and in this

---

[7] This falls outside the scope of the present work. It is the subject matter of al-Ghazālī's *Ihyā'*, and a discussion of it is to be found in Muhammad Abul Quasem, *The Ethics of al-Ghazālī: a Composite Ethics in Islam*, 2nd ed., New York, 1978, pp. 105-46.

connection is pointed out the comparative value of knowledge, devotional acts, beneficial acts and assistance to the righteousness of the righteous, and the acquisition of the necessities of life.

Having thus discussed how a man practising the beginning of guidance passes his time from waking up from sleep until returning to bed, al-Ghazālī explains the best methods of performing ritual prayer, of leading a ritual prayer, of ritual prayer in congregation, and of the Friday Assembly Prayer. He states the activities through which a pious man can devote Friday, the best day of the week in Islam, entirely to the Hereafter. This is followed by a discussion of fasting in the month of Ramaḍān, on other great days of the year, of the month and of the week. The man practising the beginning of guidance fasts not only in the month of Ramadān but also on other great days, and seeks the perfection of his fasting which consists in, in addition to abstention from eating, drinking and sexual activity, restraning the body and soul from all that is disliked by God. In this connection al-Ghazālī mentions the significance and aim of fasting and how it serves as the foundation of all devotional acts and the key to all that draws man near to God. Divine tax (*zakā*) and pilgrimage are not discussed in this book dealing with only the beginning of guidance, and the reader is advised by al-Ghazālī to consult his *Revival* for information on them. [8]

From the acts of obedience to God al-Ghazālī passes on to the acts prohibited by Him which must be avoided by one practising the beginning of guidance. He states the reason why avoidance of prohibited acts is more difficult than the performance of acts of obedience. Prohibited acts are identical with sins, and because sins are committed by different parts of the body it is these parts which must be checked. These parts are seven in number: the eyes, the ears, the tongue, the stomach, the genitals, the hands, and the feet. Al-Ghazālī states the purposes of the creation of each of these parts, enumerates the sins committed by them mentions the evils of these sins in this world and the world to come, and suggests specific methods of guarding against them. In fine he suggests certain general methods of keeping away from sins of the body. Then by demonstrating the link between man's outward self and the inward, he goes on to discuss three sins of the soul which must be removed from the soul of one practising the beginning of guidance. These sins are: envy, ostentation and pride. The reason why it is sufficient to

---

[8] Divine tax and pilgrimage are discussed in great detail in Abū Ḥāmid Muḥammad al-Ghazālī, *Iḥyā' 'Ulūm ad-Dīn*, Beirut, n.d., I, 208-30, 239-72.

get rid of only these three vices is given. Each of these vices is defined, its evil is pointed out, and the methods of its removal from the soul is suggested. A common source of these three vices is discovered in love of evil aspects of the world, which too must be removed from the soul of one practising the beginning of guidance. After drawing a conclusion on acts of obedience and sins, a trasition is made to the treatment of good manners of association with people which must be observed by those practising the beginning of guidance.

Al-Ghazālī stresses that a man practising the beginning of guidance lives a family life and a life in a community. To compensate for his shortcomings in religious duties caused by his engagement in household and social affairs he reserves part of his day or night to be alone with his Master and to enjoy the pleasure of secret converse with Him, and this special devotion he accomplishes by observing certain rules which al-Ghazālī describes in a section entitled 'Methods of Companionship with God.' This is followed by a brief treatment of different sets of good manners which a pious man observes in his companionship with different categories of people, such as teachers, students, parents and other relatives, intimate friends, those who are known but not intimately, and those who are unknown. Aside from specific sets of good manners of companionship, a general maxim of behaviour with people is also set down. This maxim is: treat them as you would like to be treated by them. Two other principles are also spoken of in various connections: the principle of abstention from causing harm to others and the principle of doing good to them in varied forms. The concept of unity and brotherhood of Muslims is emphasized.

All this concerns the requirements of the beginning of guidance or outward piety. As for the consequences of practising this guidance, they are mentioned in numerous passages scattered throughout the book. The otherworldly consequence in the form of salvation from Hell and happiness in Paradise is emphasized in agreement with Islamic religious teaching, but this-worldly consequences are not ignored for they too are given importance in the Qur'ān and Tradition.

Continuance in the practice of the beginning of guidance is a difficult task no doubt, but al-Ghazālī suggests certain methods which will facilitate this continuance. Among these methods are: to secure full control over the carnal soul (*nafs*) and to repel Satan by certain specific means, not to rely much upon divine generosity and forgiveness, and abandonment of hope of a long life. Patience is needed very much. Equally needed is a sense of the importance of time for the pious life and a careful planning of time and arranging duties from morning to evening.

The theory of the beginning of guidance or outward piety outlined above is set forth in al-Ghazālī's book, *Bidāyat al-Hidāya*, and was practised by himself, as by his disciples, in the last part of his life at Tus. This book in its entirety is translated, with a running commentary and numerous notes, in the present work in order to provide the reader with al-Ghazālī's views in full. The runing commentary set in italics and put between square brackets is placed at the start of major sections to serve as a key to the understanding of them. The footnotes are added by the translator to provide the reader with more relevant information and to augment the scholarly nature of the book. For these same reasons are added this introduction, the bibliography, indexes and so on. In translating, efforts are made to remain very close to the Arabic original and at the same time to clarify its meaning. For this clarification, material is sometimes added in the text and put between square brackets. To facilitate the reading, some expressions based on the original are put between round brackets. Qur'ānic verses are numbered according to the official Egyptian edition of the Qur'ān. The system of transliteration followed is given on page 15. It is hoped that the book will be useful to readers of English interested in the practical aspect of Islam and in al-Ghazālī. I take this opportunity to express my thanks to Mr. Peter Mooney and Dr. Harold Crouch of the National University of Malaysia for going through the manuscript before it was sent to the press and for reading the proofs.

National University of Malaysia
    Bangi, Selangor   M. Abul Quasem

Rajab 1399
June 1979

TRANSLITERATION

Consonants

ء	' (except when initial)	ز	z	ق	q
ب	b	س	s	ك	k
ت	t	ش	sh	ل	l
ث	th	ص	ṣ	م	m
ج	j	ض	ḍ	ن	n
ح	ḥ	ط	ṭ	ه	h
خ	kh	ظ	ẓ	و	w
د	d	ع	'	ي	y
ذ	dh	غ	gh		
ر	r	ف	f		

Short Vowels

‍ ◌َ : a ◌ُ : u ◌ِ : i

Long Vowels

ي ◌َ or ا ◌َ : ā　و ◌ُ : ū　ي ◌ِ : ī

Dipthongs

ي ◌َ : ay　و ◌َ : aw　وّ ◌ُ : uww　يّ ◌ِ : iyy

The letter ة is sometimes transliterated into 't' and sometimes omitted.

ABBREVIATIONS

The abbreviations listed below are used for journals and encyclopaedias mentioned in this work.

EI	—	*The Encyclopaedia of Islam* (1st edition)
EI²	—	*The Encyclopaedia of Islam* (2nd edition)
SEI	—	*The Shorter Encyclopaedia of Islam*
ERE	—	*The Encyclopaedia of Religion and Ethics*
IC	—	*The Islamic Culture*
IQ	—	*The Islamic Quarterly*
IS	—	*Islamic Studies*
JAOS	—	*Journal of the American Oriental Society*
JRAS	—	*Journal of the Royal Asiatic Society*
MW	—	*The Muslim World*
RT	—	*Revue Thomiste*
DWT	—	*Die Welt des Islam*

AL-GHAZĀLĪ ON ISLAMIC GUIDANCE

INTRODUCTION

In the name of God, Most Gracious, Ever Merciful

[*The aim of the acquistion of Islamic religious knowledge should not be the attainment of wordly things, such as wealth, reputation as a scholar, influence, boasting and rivalry; it should be action* [1] *for the attainment of otherwordly happiness.*

Islamic knowledge is meant for guidance which has a beginning and an end. First a man has to acquire knowledge of the beginning of guidance and act in accordance with it. It is only after this that he can proceed to the end of guidance.

Guidance is identical with piety (taqwa). Piety means carrying out God's orders and turning aside from His prohibitions. The beginning of guidance is the outward aspect of piety, and it is with this aspect that this book deals.]

The Shaykh, the Imām, the great scholar, the Proof of Islam (*ḥujjat al-Islām*), and the Blessing of Mankind, Abū Ḥāmid Muḥammad ibn Muḥammad ibn Muḥammad al-Ghazālī aṭ-Ṭūsī (may God sanctify his soul and illuminate his grave!) said:

Praise be to God as is His right! May the blessings and peace be upon the best of His creatures Muḥammad, and upon his family and his companions after him!

I see that with great eagerness you set out to acquire knowledge; you express that your desire for knowledge is genuine and that your thirst for it is excessive. But know that if, in your quest for knowledge, your aim is rivalry, boasting, surpassing those who are equal to you in age and merit, attraction of others' attention to you, and amassing the vanities of this world, then you are in reality trying to ruin your own religious nature and destroy yourself, to sell your [happiness of the] Hereafter for [happiness of] this life; your bargain is a dead loss, and your trading without profit. [In such a case] the teacher who is assisting you in your disobedience to God, is like one who sells a sword to a highwayman, as the Prophet (may God bless him and greet him!) said,

---

[1] For a brief discussion of this see Quasem, *Ethics*, pp. 22f.

"Whoever assists [a man] in sin, even by half a word, is his partner in it." [2]

However, if, in seeking knowledge, your intention and the purpose between God (exalted is He!) and yourself is to receive guidance and not merely to acquire information, then rejoice — the angels will spread out their wings for you when you walk [in your pursuit of knowledge], [3]   and fishes of the sea will pray [to God] for your forgiveness when you make efforts [to acquire knowledge]. [4]

At the very outset, however, you should know that guidance which is the fruit of knowledge has a beginning and an end, an outward aspect and an inward. It is not possible to reach the end except after the completion of the beginning; it is not possible to discover the inward aspect except after knowing the outward.

Take notice, [in this book] I give you counsel concerning the beginning of guidance, so that thereby you may test your carnal soul and examine your mind. If you find your mind inclined towards the beginning of guidance and your carnal soul obedient and receptive, then go ahead, look for the end, and penetrate to the bottom of the oceans of various forms of knowledge. If, however, you find that, when you meet the beginning of guidance face to face, your mind procrastinates and puts off acting in accordance with its demand, then know that your carnal soul which is inclined to seek [2] knowledge is 'that carnal soul which certainly commands you to do evil.' [5]   It has been roused in obedience to Satan, the accursed, in order that he may lower you into the well by the rope of his deception, and by his wiles bring you gradually to the abyss of destruction. His aim is to press his evil wares upon you in the place where good wares are sold, so that he may unite you with 'those who are the greatest losers in respect of their works, whose efforts in this life have gone astray, though they imagine that they are producing excellent works.' [6]   In order to deceive you, Satan calls your attention to the excellence of knowledge and the high rank of the learned [in Paradise] and to the statements of pious men as well as the prophetic traditions on these; he diverts your attention from the following sayings of the Prophet (may God bless him and greet him!) which urge men to transform their knowledge into action:

[2] Ibn Māja, *Sunan*, Diyyāt, 1 (with variation).

[3] *Ibid.*, Muqaddama, 17; Abū Dāwūd, *Sunan*, 'Ilm, 1; at-Tirmidhī, *Sunan*, 'Ilm, 19; an-Nasā'ī, *Sunan*, Ṭahāra, 112; Ibn Ḥanbal, *Musnad*, IV, 239ff., V, 192.

[4] Cf. at-Tirmudhī, *Sunan*, 'Ilm, 17; Abū Dāwūd, *Sunan*, 'Ilm, 1.

[5] Qur'ān 12:53.   [6] Qur'ān 18:103-104.

"Whoever increases in knowledge and does not increase in guidance, only increases in distance from God. [7]

The most severe punishment on the Day of Judgement will be that of a learned man who did not derive benefit from his knowledge [by acting in accordance with it]. [8]

God, I seek the protection of Youagainst knowledge which does not benefit, against the mind which does not humble itself, against the action which is not lifted up to God, and against the supplication which is not accepted by Him. [9]

During the night in which I was carried [to the near presence of God] [10] I passed by some groups of people whose lips were cut by fiery scissors. I asked them,'Who are you?' They replied, 'We are those who used to advise others to do good and yet ourselves did not do it, and used to prohibit others from doing evil and yet ourselves did it.' " [11]

Beware, then, O unfortunate man, of listening to the fair words of Satan, lest he lower you into the well by the rope of his deception.

Woe to the ignorant man once, for he has not acquired knowledge! But woe to the learned man a thousand times, for he has not acted in accordance with what he learned!

Know that people who seek knowledge are of three types. 1. There is the man who seeks knowledge as a provision for the life to come. By seeking knowledge he intends only the glorious face of God and the happiness of the Hereafter. Such a man is one of those who will be successful in the Hereafter.

2. There is the man who seeks knowledge for the help it gives in his transitory life in this world to obtain power, influence and wealth; yet he is aware of the worthlessness of his condition and the meanness of his aim. Such a man is in jeopardy. If his appointed term [i.e. death] comes upon him before he repents, a bad end (*sū' al-khātima*) to his life [12] is to be feared for him and his fate will depend upon the will of God. If, however, God gives him grace to

---

[7] Ibn Ḥanbal, *Musnad*, II, 371, 441.

[8] Cf. ad-Dārimī, *Sunan*, Muqaddama, 27.

[9] Muslim, *Ṣaḥīḥ*, Dhikr, 73; Abū Dāwūd, *Sunan*, Witr, 32; an-Nasā'ī, *Sunan*, Isti'ādha, 13, 18, 21, 64; at-Tirmidhī, *Sunan*, Da'wāt, 68; Ibn Māja *Sunan*, Muqaddama, 23, Du'ā', 2f.; Ibn Ḥanbal, *Musnad*, II, 168, 198, IV, 371, 381.

[10] Qur'ān 17:1.   [11] Ibn Ḥanbal, *Musnad*, II, 120, 231, 239.

[12] For a discussion of the bad end to life see al-Ghazālī, *Iḥyā'*, IV, 173-80.

repent before the arrival of the appointed term, and he adds action to his knowledge and makes up for the action he neglected, he will join those who will be successful in the Hereafter, for

> 'The man who repents of sin is like the man who has no sin.' [13]

3. The third man has been overcome by Satan. He has made his knowledge a means to increase his wealth, to boast of his influence and to pride himself on his numerous followers. By his knowledge he explores every avenue which offers a prospect of realizing that for which he hopes from this world. Despite this, he feels that he has a high status with God, and with his garb and jargon he bears the brand and stamp of learned men along with his mad desire of this world openly and secretly. Such a man is among those who will be destroyed in the Hereafter and is one of those who are stupid and deluded in this world, for there is no hope for his repentance since he imagines that he is one of the gooddoers. He is unmindful of the words of God (exalted is He!):

> "O you who believe, why do you say that which you do not do?" [14] (ياايهاالذين امنوا لم تقولون مالا تفعلون؟)

This man belongs to that group of people concerning whom the Messenger of God (may God bless him and greet him!) said,

> "For you I fear one who is not the Antichrist (*Dajjāl*) more than I fear the Antichrist." Someone asked him, "Who is that, O the Messenger of God?" He replied, "An evil scholar."

The reason for this is that the aim of the Antichrist [3] is to lead men astray. The evil scholar, although he turns men from this world by his words and speech, calls them to it by his actions and states. [It is a fact that] a man's actions and states speak more eloquently than his words and speech; human nature is more inclined to share in actions than to follow words and statements. The corruption which the deluded scholar causes with his actions is greater than the improvement he effects by his words; for the ignorant man does not venture to set his desire on the world till the scholars have done so. Thus the scholar's knowledge becomes a cause of God's servants venturing to disobey Him. Despite this his ignorant soul feels presumtuous; he is filled   with expectation and hope of divine

---

[13] Ibn Māja, *Sunan*, Zuhd, 30.   [14] Qur'ān 61:2.

favour, and this leads him to feel that by his knowledge he has done favour to God, and this suggests to him that he is better than many people.

Be, then, of the first group, O seeker after God. Guard against being of the second group, for many a procrastinator is suddenly overtaken by his appointed term [i.e. death] before repenting, and becomes a loser. But beware, I repeat, beware of being in the third group and of destroying utterly [in the Hereafter] without any hope of your prosperity there.

You may ask: What is the beginning of guidance in order that I may test my carnal soul thereby?

[As a reply to this question] know that the beginning of guidance is outward piety and the end of guidance is inward piety. Only through piety good consequences can be achieved, and only the pious are guided. Piety means carrying out the commands of God (exalted is He!) and turning aside from all that He prohibits, and thus has two parts. Take notice that in this book I give you counsel by a brief explanation of the outward aspect of piety in both its parts.

PART ONE

ACTS OF DEVOTION

PREAMBLE

[The commands of God prescribe both obligatory and supererogatory acts of devotion. A man should perform both categories of acts, and he can do so only if he carefully plans his time and arranges his duties from the morning to evening, and is very diligent in executing his plan. This plan, this arrangement, is suggested in all chapters of this part of this book.]

Know that God's commands (exalted is He!) prescribe obligatory acts and supererogatory acts. The obligatory acts are the capital on which trading activities are based, and it is through them that man achieves salvation [in the Hereafter]. The supererogatory acts are the profit, and it is through these that higher degrees of success can be achieved in the world to come. The Prophet (may God bless him and greet him!) said,

> "God (blessed and exalted is He!) says, 'Nothing brings men near to Me like the performance of that which I made obligatory for them, and through supererogatory acts My servant [i.e. man] comes even nearer to Me until I love him. When I have bestowed My love on him, I become his hearing with which he hears, his sight with which he sees, his tongue with which he speaks, his hand with which he grasps, and his feet with which he walks.' " [15]

Never can you, O novice, arrive at the state of fulfilling the commands of God unless you watch over the [activities of your] mind and the members of your body every single moment from morning to night. Know that God (exalted is He!) is aware of your mind, that He observes your outward self (*ẓāhir*) and the inward (*bāṭin*), that He comprehends your every glance, your every thought, your every step, and your every other form of movement and state of being at

[15] Al-Bukhārī, *Ṣaḥīḥ*, Riqāq, 38.

23

rest, and that, whether you are in association with other people or in seclusion, you live constantly in His presence. In the world of perception and the unseen world no inactive thing remains inactive and no moving thing moves, except with the Most Compelling One [16] of the heavens and the earth being aware of these [4]. [17]

> "He [i.e. God] knows the treachery of the eyes and that which the mind conceals. [18] He knows all that is secret and most hidden." [19]

(يعلم خائنة الأعين، وما تخفى الصــدورة ويعلم السر وأخفى)

So, O poor man, make your behaviour, both inward and outward, in the presence of God (exalted is He!) like the behaviour of the lowly and erring slave in the presence of a most compelling and subduing king. Try hard so that your Master may not see you where He forbade you to be and may not miss you where He commanded you to be. [20] You will never be able to do this, unless you plan your time and arrange your duties from morning to evening. From the moment you wake from sleep until the time of your returning to your bed, be diligent in performing the commands God (exalted is He!) lays upon you.

PRAISEWORTHY WAY OF WAKING FROM SLEEP

[How a believer should wake from sleep is discussed in this section. Observance of the suggestions made here will make him a good believer, a religious man of the higher grade. Disregard of them is, of course, not a sin.]

In waking from sleep, try to wake before dawn. Let the first thing which comes to your mind and tongue be the remembrance of God and praise of Him. So at the time of waking, supplicate:

> Praise be to God Who has made us alive after making us [i.e. our sensations] dead [21] [in sleep], and towards Whom is the return [after death]. [22] We and the rest of creation belong to God in this morning; greatness and authority belong to Him; might and power belong to Him, the Lord of all the worlds. In this morning we are at the state of natural

16 Qur'ān 59:23.

17 Comparison of these last two sentences with the second passage of the third part of this book shows that this part is authentic, not spurious.

18 Qur'ān 4:20.   19 Qur'ān 20:6.

20 This means that man must neither do anything God prohibited him to do, nor leave undone anything God commanded him to do.

21 Qur'ān 39:42.   22 Qur'ān 67:15.

disposition of Islam, [23] on the Statement of Sincerity [24] [which is: 'There is no god but God'], on the religion of our prophet Muḥammad (may God bless him and greet him!), and on the religion of our father Abraham, a man of pure faith, a man completely surrendered to God and was not one of those who believe that God has divine partners. [25] God, we pray to You that You would direct us today to all good. I seek the protection of You from committing any evil today and from bringing any evil upon a Muslim. God, through You alone we have come to this morning, through You alone we passed the night, through You alone we live, through You alone we die, and to You alone is our final return. [26] We pray to You for the good of today and of that which is in it; we seek the protection of You from the evil of today and of that which is in it.

(الحمدلله الذى احيانا بعد ما اماتنا۴ واليه النشور. اصبحنا واصبح الملك لله۴ والعظمة والسلطان لله۴ والعزة والقدرة لله رب‌العالمين. اصبحنا على فطرة الاسلام۴ وعلى كلمة الاخلاص۴ وعلى دين نبينا محمد صلى الله عليه وسلم۴ وعلى ملة ابينا ابراهيم حنيفا مسلما وماكان من المشركين. اللهم۴ انا نسالك ان تبعثنا فى هذا اليوم الى كل خير۴ واعوذ بك ان اجترح فيه سوأ اواجره الى مسلم. اللهم۴ بك اصبحنا وبك امسينا وبك نحيا وبك نموت واليك النشور. نسالك خير هذا اليوم وخير ما فيه۴ ونعوذ بك من شر هذا اليوم وشر ما فيه).

When you put on your clothes [after waking from sleep], produce in your mind the intention of fulfilling the commands of God (exalted is He!) to cover your private parts. Beware of making your purpose in wearing clothes to dissemble before others; if this be your purpose you will be the loser.

PROPER METHODS OF ENTERING THE LAVATORY

[*On waking from sleep when a believer habitually goes to lavatory he should follow certain methods in relieving himself. These methods are mentioned in this section.*]

[23] This refers to the oft-quoted Qur'ānic verse 30:30.

[24] Qur'ān 3:64, 48:26, 14:24.

[25] Qur'ān 2:135, 30:67f., 95, 4:125, 6:161, 16:120, 123.   [26] Qur'ān 6:162, 67:15.

When you go to the lavatory to relieve yourself, enter with the left foot first and come out with the right foot first. [27] Do not take with you anything containing the name of God (exalted is He!) or of His Messenger. Do not enter bare-headed or bare-footed. When entering the lavatory supplicate:

> In the name of God; I seek the protection of God from filth and defilement, from soiling impurity, from Satan, the accursed. [28]

(بسم الله. اعوذ بالله من الرجس النجس الخبيث المخبث الشيطان الرجيم)

When coming out of the lavatory supplicate:

> God, I seek forgiveness from You. Praise be to God Who has caused me to remove that which would harm me and to leave in me that which will benefit me!

(غفرانك. الحمد لله الذى اذهب عنى مايو ذينى، وابقى على ماينفعنى)

You should make ready the pebbles [or paper for cleansing] before relieving yourself, and should not cleanse yourself with water in [5] the closet itself. When you pass water, you should seek freedom from it by a sort of half-cough and sprinkling three times and by placing the left hand under the penis.

If you are in the desert, go away from the eyes of those who can see you, and veil yourself from them with some object if there is one. Do not expose your private parts before reaching the place where you are to squat to relieve yourself. Do not face the direction of the Holy Ka'ba in Mecca, [29] and do not turn either face or back to sun or moon. Do not pass water in a place where people meet, nor in still water, nor under a tree with fruits, nor in a hole. Avoid hard ground and the windward direction so that you are not splashed, for the Prophet (may God bless him and greet him!) said,

> "Generally, the punishment of the grave is from the sprinkles of urine." [30]

[27] Since the right hand and right foot are more excellent than the left, they should be used in superior acts. To leave the lavatory, a place of filth, is an act superior to entering it; hence it is better to enter with the left foot first and to come out with the right foot first.

[28] Cf. al-Bukhārī, *Ṣaḥīḥ*, Waḍū', 9; at-Tirmidhī, *Sunan*, Ṭahāra, 4; Ibn Māja, *Sunan*, Ṭahāra, 9.

[29] This is prohibited by the Prophet. See Ibn Mājā, *Sunan*, Ṭahāra, 16.

[30] Al-Bukhārī, *Ṣaḥīḥ*, Janā'iz, 88; Ibn Ḥanbal, *Musnad*, V, 36.

In squatting, rest upon your left foot. Do not urinate standing, except when there is a severe necessity.

In cleansing yourself use both stone [or hard soil or paper] and water. Should you want to limit yourself to one, water is preferable. If you confine yourself to stone [or hard soil or paper] only, you must use three clean dry pieces, wiping the anus with them in such a way that no other part of the body is soiled by the ordure. Similarly, wipe the penis on three sides of a stone [or a piece of paper]. If it is not completely cleansed after three times, wipe five or seven, so that cleansing is completed after an odd number of times. The odd is praiseworthy [31] ; cleansing is required. Cleanse yourself only with the left hand. On finishing the cleansing, supplicate:

> God, cleanse my mind from hypocrisy and protect my genitals from adultery. [32]

(اللهم، طهر قلبى من النفاق، وحصن فرجى من الفواحش)

After completing the cleansing, rub your hand on the earth or on a wall [or on soap], and then wash it.

RULES OF ABLUTION (*WAḌŪ'*)

[On coming out of the lavatory before sunrise, a Muslim washes his hands, face and feet, following certain specific rules. This is called ablution or ritual purification, and it is through this that he prepares himself for the Dawn Prayer. Some of these rules are necessary for the validity of ablution, while others only increase its merit. A pious Muslim observes all these rules and thus perfects his ritual purification. Ablution is necessary not only for all ritual prayers, but also for certain other Islamic religious acts, such as Qur'ān-reading by touching the Qur'ān.]

1. After you have finished cleansing yourself, [following the methods described in the preceding chapter], do not omit the use of a tooth-stick (*miswāk*), for its use cleanses the mouth, pleases the Lord, and displeases Satan. [The Prophet said,]

> "A ritual prayer performed after the use of a tooth-stick is better than seventy ritual prayers performed without its use." [33]

---

[31] Not only here but also in many other cases, an odd number is praiseworthy, because there is a Tradition: "God is odd [in number] and He likes the odd number." See al-Bukhārī, *Ṣaḥīḥ*, Da'wāt, 69; Muslim, *Ṣaḥīḥ*, Dhikr, 5f.; at-Tirmidhī, *Sunan*, Witr, 2.   [33] Aḥmad ibn Ḥanbal, *Musnad*, 169.

[32] Cf. Abū Ṭālib al-Makkī, *Qūt al-Qulūb*, Cairo, 1961, II, 184.

It is related from Abū Hurayra [34] (may God be pleased with him!) that God's Messenger (may God bless him and greet him!) said,

> "Had it not been for my fear to overburden my people, I would have commanded them to use the tooth-stick before every ritual prayer." [35]

The prophet (may God bless him and greet him!) also said,

> "I was commanded so much to use the tooth-stick that I feared that it would be made obligatory on me." [36]

2. After cleansing the mouth with the tooth-stick, sit for ablution in a raised place, facing the direction of the Ka'ba in Mecca, so that the splashes do not reach you, and supplicate:

> In the name of God, Most Gracious Ever Merciful. 'Lord, I seek the protection of You against the incitements of Satans, and I seek the protection of You, Lord, lest they should approach me.' [37]

(بسم الله الرحمن الرحيم. اعوذ بك مـن همزات الشياطين، واعوذبكم ربم ان يحضرون).

3. Then wash your hands three times before placing them in the basin, and supplicate:

> God, I pray to You for good fortune and blessing, and I seek the protection of You from ill luck and disaster. [38]

(اللهم، انى اسالك اليمن والبركـة، واعـوذ بك مـن الـشوم والهلكة)

4. Then produce in your mind the intention (*niyya*) that your ablution is for removing uncleanliness or for making you fit for the ritual prayer. The production of intention should not be [6] omitted before washing the face, for otherwise your ablution is invalid.

Then take a handful of water for your mouth and rinse your mouth three times, making sure that the water reaches the back of it

---

[34] Abū Hurayra (d. 58 or 59 A.H.) was a famous companion of the Prophet and a prolific narrator of Tradition. For an account of him see Ibn Ḥajar al-'Asqalānī, *al-Isāba*, IV, 200-208; Ibn 'Abd al-Barr, *al-Istī'āb* in Ibn Ḥajar, *op. cit.*, IV, 200-207.

[35] Aḥmad ibn Ḥanbal. *Musnad*, I, 80, 120, 170; al-Bukhārī, *Ṣaḥīḥ*, Jumu'a, 8; Muslim, *Ṣaḥīḥ*, Ṭahāra, 42.

[36] Ibn Ḥanbal, *Musnad*, I, 237, 285, III, 490.

[37] Qur'ān 33:99f. This supplication formula is also cited in al-Makkī's *Qūt*, II, 184.

[38] Cf. al-Makkī, *Qūt* II, 184 where the same formula of prayer is to be found.

— if, however, you are fasting do this act very gently, [lest the water should go to the stomach] — and supplicate:

> God, help me to read Your Book [i.e. the Qur'ān] and to remember You enormously; 'strengthen me, in this world and the Hereafter, with the Statement [i.e. 'there is no god but God'] that is firmly established.' [39]

(اللهم اعنى على تلاوة كتابك وكثرة الذكر لك وثبتنى بالقول الثابت فى الحياة الدنيا وفى الاخرة)

5. Then take a handful of water for your nose, draw it in three times, and blow out the moisture in your nose. While drawing it in, supplicate:

> God, make me breathe in the fragrance of Paradise, and be pleased with me. [40]

(اللهم ارحنى رائحة الجنة وانت عنى راض)

While blowing the water out of the nose, supplicate:

> God, I seek the protection of You from the odours of Hell and from the evil abode [i.e. Hell]. [41]

(اللهم انى اعوذ بك من روائح النار وسوء الدار)

6. Then take a handful of water for your face and with it wash from the beginning of the flattening of the forehead to the end of the protuberance of the chin, up and down, and from ear to ear across. Make the water reach the place of *tahdhīf*, which is the point from which women customarily remove the hair and is that place which lies between the top of the ear and the corner of the temples, I mean, that area which is situated between them. Make the water reach the four places where hair grows: the eye-brows, the moustache, the eye-lashes and the cheeks, i.e. that place which lies in front of the ears from the beginning of the beard. The water must also reach the roots of the hair of the thin part of the beard, but not of the thick part. When you wash your face supplicate:

> God, make my face bright through your light on the Day of Judgement, when You will brighten the faces of Your friends, and do not blacken my face with darkness on the

[39] Qur'ān 14:27. Only the first part of this formula is cited in al-Makkī's *Qūt*, II, 184.

[40] Al-Makkī, however, cited (*Qūt*, II, 184) this formula with a slight addition in the beginning.

[41] This has also been cited by a-Makkī in his *Qūt*, II, 184.

Day of Judgement, when You will blacken the faces of Your enemies. [42]

(اللهم؛ بيض وجهي بنورك يوم تبيض وجوه اوليائك؛ ولاتسود وجهي بظلماتك يوم تسود وجوه اعدائك).

Do not omit wetting the thick part of the beard.

7. Then wash your right hand, and after that the left, together with the elbow and half the upper arm; for the adornment in Paradise will reach to the places touched in ablution. When washing your right hand pray:

> God, give me my record of action in my right hand, and grant me an easy reckoning. [43]

(اللهم؛ اعطني كتابي بيميني؛ وحاسبني حسابا يسيرًا)

When washing the left hand pray:

> God, I seek the protection of You from being given my record of action in my left hand or behind my back. [44]

(اللهم؛ انى اعوذبك ان تعطيني كتابي بشمالى اومـــن وراء ظهري)

8. Then, moistening your hands, wipe all over your head, keeping the finger-tips of right and left hands close together, placing them on the fore part of the head and moving them back to the nape of the neck and then forward again. Do this thrice — as you wash the other limbs of the body thrice — and pray:

> God, cover me with Your mercy, send down Your blessings upon me, and shelter me beneath the shadow of Your throne 'on the Day of Judgement when there will be no shadow except Yours.' [45] God, make my hair and my flesh forbidden things in Hell. [46]

(اللهم؛ غشني برحمتك؛ وانزل على من بركاتك؛ واظلني تحت ظل عرشك يوم لاظل الاظلك. اللهم؛ حرم شعرى وبشرى على النار)

---

[42] Qur'ān 3:106.

[43] This refers to Qur'ān 17:71, 69:19, 84:7. Cf. al-Makkī, *Qūt*, II, 184 where the same formula is to be found.

[44] This has reference to Qur'ān 19:20, 84:10. This formula has also been cited in al-Makkī's *Qūt*,, II, 184.

[45] For the absence of shadows except God's see al-Bukhārī, *Ṣaḥīḥ*, Adhān, 36; Abū Dāwūd, *Sunan*, Sunna, 1f.; an-Nasā'ī, *Sunan*, Īmān, 2ff., Quḍāt, 2; at-Tirmidhī, *Sunan*, Zuhd, 53.

[46] This last sentence is omitted in al-Makkī's *Qūt*, II, 184.

9. Then wipe your ears, outside and inside with fresh water; place your forefingers in your earholes and wipe the outside of your ears with the ball of your thumbs, and pray:

> God, make me one of those who listen to the Word and follow the best in it. [47] God, make me hear the call of the caller of Paradise along with the pious in Paradise. [48]

(اللهم اجعلنى من الذين يستمعون القول، فيتبعون احسنه.
اللهم اسمعنى منادى الجنة فى الجنة مع الابرار)

10. Then wipe your neck, and pray:

> 'God, deliver my neck from Hell. I seek the protection of You from the iron collars [which will be round the poly-theists' necks] and from the chains with which they will be dragged into the boiling water of Hell]. [49]

(اللهم فك رقبتى من النار، واعوذ بك من السلاسل والاغلال)

11. Then wash [7] your right foot, and after that the left, together with the ankles. With the little finger of your left hand wash between your toes, beginning with the little toe of your right foot and finishing with the little toe of your left; approach the toes from below and supplicate:

> God, establish my feet on the straight path along with the feet of Your righteous servants. [50]

(اللهم، ثبت قدمى على الصراط المستقيم مع اقدام عبادك الصالحين)

Similarly when you wash your left foot, supplicate:

> God, I seek the protection of You that You may not cause my feet to slip from the Bridge-like path [to be suspended over Hell] into the gulf of Hell on the Day of Judgement when You will cause the feet of the hypocrites and poly-theists to slip. [51]

(اللهم، انى اعوذبك ان تزل قدمى على الصراط فى النار يوم تزل اقدام المنافقين والمشركين)

Bring the water above your ankles. Be careful to repeat all your

---

[48] Cf. al-Makkī, *Qūt*, II, 184. [47] Qur'ān 39:18.

[49] Reference is to Qur'ān 40:71. Al-Makkī (*Qūt*, II, 184) has also cited this formula in its entirety.

[50] Cf. Qur'ān 1:6-7, 2:142; al-Makkī, *Qūt*, II, 184 where this formula prayer is mentioned with a slight variation.

[51] Cf. Qur'ān 37:23; al-Makkī, *Qūt*, II, 184.

actions of ablution three times.

12. When you have finished your ablution raise your eyes to the heaven and say:

> I bear witness that there is no god except God alone; He has no partner. I [also] bear witness that Muḥammad is His servant and messenger. God, Holy are You and praise be to You!
>
> I bear witness that there is no god except You. I have done evil and thus have done wrong to myself; so I seek forgiveness from You and I turn to You in repentance; forgive me and turn to me in mercy, for most certainly You are Oft-returning with compassion, Ever Merciful.
>
> God, make me one of those who turn to You very often, make me one of those who are clean and pure, [52] make me one of Your righteous servants, [53] make me patient and grateful, and make me such as is able to remember You enormously and to extol Your glory morning and evening.

(اشهد ان لا اله الا الله وحـده لاشريك له، واشهد ان محمدا عبده ورسوله. سـبحانك، اللهم، وبحمدك. اشهد ان لا اله الا انت. عملت سوأ وظلمت نفسى، استغفرك واتوب اليك. فاغفرلى وتب على، انك انت التواب الرحيم. اللهـم، اجعلني من التوابين، واجعلنى من المتطهرين، واجعلنى من عبادك الصالحين، واجعلني صبورا شكورا، واجعلنى اذكرك ذكرا كثيرا واسبحك بكرة واصيلا)[54]

If a man says these supplications during his ablution, his sins depart from all his limbs, a seal is set on his ablution, it is raised to beneath the throne of God and unceasingly glorifies Him and hallows Him, and the reward of that ablution is recorded for him to the Day of Resurrection. [55]

Avoid seven things in your ablution. 1. Do not shake your hands much so as to splash the water. 2. Do not strike the water against your head and face noisily. 3. Do not talk during the ablution. 4. Do not wash an organ more than three times. 5. Do not, through mere scrupulosity, pour more water than is necessary, for the scrupulous have a Satan called the Walhān who plays with them.

---

[52] Qur'ān 2:222. [53] Qur'ān 27:19.

[54] Qur'ān 33:42, 48-9, 76:25. Al-Makkī (Qūt, II, 184f.) has also cited this prayer formula.

[55] This passage also occurs in al-Makkī's Qūt II, 185.

6. Do not perform your ablution with water lain in the sun. 7. Do not use copper vessels. These seven things are disliked by God (*makrūh*) in ablution.

We find a Tradition:

> "If a man remembers God at his ablution, God purifies his whole body; if a man does not remember God, He purifies only those parts of him where the water has reached."

RULES OF WASHING THE BODY

[A Muslim who has become physically unclean and who wants to perform ritual prayer, to read the Qur'ān, or to do certain other religious duties, must clean himself by washing the entire body (ghusl) in the Islamic way. [56] *In this form of cleanliness also, certain things are obligatory for everyone, while others are of less importance but should not be neglected by one who desires to be among those who are drawn near to God.]*

If you have incurred the major impurity from nocturnal emission or sexual intercourse, carry a basin to the wash-place and [1] wash your hands first of all three times, [2] remove any defilement from your body, and [3] perform ablution in the same way as you do it before ritual prayer [as described in the preceding chapter] together with the recitation of all relevant supplications, but postpone the washing of the feet, so as not to waste the water.

[4] When you have finished the ablution, pour water over your head three times, [5] while producing in your mind the intention that you are washing your body in order to remove the defilement of major impurity.

[6] Then pour water over the right side of your body three times, and then over the left side of your body three times. [8]. Rub front and back of your body. Pick the hair of your head and beard with wet fingers. Make the water reach the bendings of the body and the roots of the hair, both thin and thick. Avoid touching your genitals after the ablution you have made for washing the body; if your hand comes in contact with them, repeat the ablution.

Of all these activities of washing the body the obligatory things are: [1] the production of ritual intention in the mind, [2] removal of defilement from the body, [3] and the washing of the body in its entirety.

Obligatory things in ablution which is part of washing the body

[56] Qur'ān 5:6.

are: washing of face and hands including the elbows, wiping of part of the head with a wet hand, the washing of the feet to the ankles, performance of each of these activities once, together with producing the intention of ablution and the observance of the correct order of these activities.

All activities of washing other than the obligatory ones [just mentioned] are emphasized sunna (*sunna mu'akkada*), which ensure much merit and great reward. The man who neglects them is the loser; indeed he endangers his basic obligatory activities of washing; for the supererogatory acts mend the obligatory ones.

RULES OF CLEANLINESS WITH SAND [*TAYAMMUM*]

[Sometimes a man is unable to make use of water for performing ablution or for washing the entire body. For such a man, Islam has made cleanliness easy by allowing him to use clean sand. [57] *The methods of using sand as a substitute for ablution and for washing the entire body are the same.*]

If you are unable to make use of water for cleanliness — either because you cannot find water after looking for it, or because you have an excuse resulting from illness, or because you are prevented from reaching water by wild beasts or by imprisonment, or because the water you have is needed to satisfy the thirst of yourself or of your friends, or because the water is the property of someone who sells it at more than proper price, or because you have such a wound or illness that if you use the water, there is fear for your life — then wait until the time of the obligatory ritual prayer comes.

[When the time comes] look for some good ground with clean, pure, smooth soil; strike it with your palms keeping your fingers closed together; 1. produce in your mind the intention that you are doing this cleanliness in order to make yourself fit for the obligatory ritual prayer; 2. wipe your face with both palms, [containing sand], once; you are not required to make the sand reach the roots of your hair, either thick or thin.

3. Then take off your ring, strike the sand a second time with your palms while spreading out the fingers; wipe your both hands including the elbows with the palms [containing some sand]. If the whole area of the hands including the elbows is not wiped, strike the sand with your palms another time and wipe the hands; do this until the whole area of the hands is wiped.

[57] Qur'ān 4:43, 5:6.

4. Then wipe one of your palms with the other, and wipe the spaces between your fingers.

[Thus your cleanliness with sand is complete], and with this cleanliness perform only one obligatory ritual prayer and as many supererogatory ritual prayers [attached with that obligatory one] as you please. If you want to perform a second obligatory ritual prayer, start another cleanliness ritual with sand from the beginning.

GOOD METHOD OF GOING TO THE MOSQUE

[*On completing cleanliness at dawn, a pious Muslim performs the first part of the Dawn Prayer at home and then proceeds to the mosque to perform the remaining part in congregation. His walk to the mosque, his intention, and his mental states are all in the path of God.*]

When you have completed your cleanliness, perform in your house the two sunna *rak'as* of the Dawn Prayer (*Ṣalāt al-Fajr*), if the dawn has already broken. The Messenger of God (may God bless him and greet him!) used to do this. Then proceed towards the mosque. Do not omit ritual prayer in congregation, especially the Dawn Prayer. Ritual prayer in congregation is twenty seven times better than the ritual prayer one performs alone. [58] If you are easy-going concerning a [spiritual] gain of this kind, what benefit will you have in seeking knowledge? Certainly the fruit of knowledge is action in accordance with it.

When [9] you walk to the mosque, walk easily and calmly, and do not hurry. When walking along the road to the mosque, supplicate:

> God, by those who beseech You and by those who long for You, and by this walk of mine to You, I swear to You that I set out neither lightheartedly nor bewildered, neither from ostentation nor from desire to be well spoken of. On the contrary, I have set out for fear of Your anger and seeking Your pleasure. I beg from You that You deliver me from Hell and forgive my sins, for there is no one who can forgive sins except You.

(اللهم، بحق السائلين عليك وبحق الـراغـبـين اليك وبحق ممشـاى هذا اليكم فانى لم اخرج اشرا ولا بطرا ولا ريـاً ولاسـمعة بل خرجت أتقاء سـخطك وابتفاء مرضاتك. فأسألك أن تـنقذنى من النار، وان تغفرلى ذنوبى، فانه لايففر الذنوب الا أنت)

[58] Al-Bukhārī, *Ṣaḥīḥ*, Adhān, 29; Muslim, *Ṣaḥīḥ*, Masjid, 245ff.

RIGHT METHODS OF ENTERING THE MOSQUE AND ACTIVITIES INSIDE IT

[Performance of obligatory parts of ritual prayer in the mosque is better than their performance at home or in other places. The mind of a really pious Muslim, wherever he may be physically, remains attached to the mosque. At the approach of the time of a ritual prayer, he hastens to the mosque and, when and after entering it, does certain obligatory and supererogatory deeds; in the case of the Dawn Prayer he spends the time between this prayer and the sunrise doing four meritorious things. The obligatory things ensure safety from Hell; the supererogatory things elevate his spiritual status.]

When you are about to enter the mosque, do so with your right foot first, and supplicate:

> God, bless Muḥammad, his family and his companions, and greet them all. God, forgive my sins and open to me the doors of Your mercy.

(اللهمّ صلّ على محمد وعلى آل محمد وصحبه وسلم. اللهمّ اغفرلى ذنوبى، وافتح لى أبواب رحمتك)

Whenever you see anyone selling anything in the mosque, [disapprove of it] saying 'May God make your trafficking unprofittable!' When you see in the mosque someone crying for a thing he lost, [try to stop him by] saying , 'May God not restore your lost thing!' The Messenger of God (may God bless him and greet him!) has commanded to say this.

When you have entered the mosque do not sit down until you pray the two *rak'as* of greeting the mosque. If you have not yet performed ablution or do not want to do so, performance of other "lasting good actions" (*al-bāqiyāt aṣ-ṣāliḥāt*) [59] [i.e. utterance of such phrases as 'praise be to God!', 'glory be to God!'] three times will suffice. Some authorities have said that these phrases need to be uttered [not three times but] four times. Some other authorities maintain that one who has not performed ablution has to utter them three times; and one who has already performed it, needs to utter them once. If you have not already performed the two sunna *rak'as* of the Dawn Prayer [at home], execute them [in the mosque] instead of the two *rak'as* of greeting the mosque; [in this case you need not perform the two *rak'as* of greeting the mosque].

When you have completed the two sunna *rak'as* of the Dawn

[59] Qur'ān 18:46.

Prayer, produce in your mind the intention of *i'tikāf* (seclusion in the mosque for complete devotion to God), and supplicate by reciting that which God's Messenger (may God bless him and greet him!) used to recite after the two sunna *rak'as* of the Dawn Prayer. So supplicate:

> God, I beseech You for Your mercy to guide my mind, to settle my affairs, to order my disorder, to repel temptation, to improve my religious nature, to preserve my secret thoughts, to raise up my visible acts, to purify my actions, to brighten my face, to inspire me to have the right direction, to satisfy all my needs, and to keep me from all evil.
>
> God, I beseech You for pure faith which will fill my mind. I beseech You for truly sure faith so that I may know that nothing will ever befall me except that which You have written down for me, and [I beseech You] for satisfaction in that which You have allotted to me. God, I beseech You for true faith, for sure faith, after which no unbelief [will enter my mind]. I also beseech You for Your mercy by which I may receive the privilege of Your regard in this world and in the Hereafter.
>
> God, I beseech You for patience with that which You have allotted to me, for success at the time of encountering You [on the Day of Judgement], for the high ranks of the martyrs [in Paradise], for the life of those who will be happy [in the Hereafter], for help against enemies, and for the companionship of the prophets [in the highest grade of Paradise].
>
> God, I place my needs before You, although my thought is weak and I fall short in my action; I am in dire need of Your mercy. I, therefore, beseech You, O Determiner of all affairs, O Healer of human souls, that, as You rescue from the midst of the seas, You would rescue me from the punishment of Hell, punishment of the grave, and the prayer for total annihilation [which the dwellers of Hell will do when they being chained will be thrown into a narrow corner of it]. [60]
>
> God, the Lord of all the worlds, I pray to You and beseech You for that good which You have promised to any man, or for that good which You bestow upon any of Your creatures, but my mind is too weak to think of it, my action

[60] This refers to Qur'ān 25:13f, 84:11.

is too imperfect to achieve it, [10] and my intention and desire could not reach it.

God, make us those who guide others to the right path and are themselves rightly guided, and not those who have themselves erred and led others astray; those who are at war with Your enemies, but at peace with Your friends; those who love men with Your love and are hostile with Your hostility towards those of Your creatures who have disobeyed You. God, this is my prayer, but it is for You to answer; this is my utmost endeavour, but in You is my trust. 'Surely we belong to God, and surely we shall return to Him.'[61] There is no ability or power except with God, the All-high, the All-great.

God, I beseech You to protect me on the Day of Doom and to grant me Paradise on the Day of Eternity, along with the saints and martyrs who bow down and fall prostrate in ritual prayer very often[62] and those who fulfil their covenants with You. Surely You are Ever Merciful, Ever Loving, and You do what You will. Glory be to Him Who is characterized by might and holds it! Glory be to Him Who is clothed and adorned with glory! Glory be to Him Who alone deserves the perfect glorification! Glory be to the Lord of bounty and grace! Glory be to the Lord of power and generosity! Glory be to Him Who has encompassed everything with His knowledge!

God, grant me light in my mind, light in my grave, light in my ears, light in my eyes, light in my hair, light in my skin, light in my flesh, light in my blood, light in my bones, light before me, light behind me, light to right of me, light to left of me, light above me, and light beneath me. God, increase my light and give me the greatest light of all.[63] Through Your mercy grant me light, O the Most Merciful of those who show mercy.[64]

When you have finished the above mentioned supplication, do not engage yourself in anything except the performance of the obligatory [two *rak'as* of the] Dawn Prayer or any form of praise of God (*dhikr*) or glorification of God (*tasbīḥ*) or recitation of the Qur'ān. If,

[61] Qur'ān 2:156.   [62] Qur'ān 2:125, 22:26, 48:29.

[63] This supplication for light was made regularly by the Prophet himself. See Muslim, *Ṣaḥīḥ*, Musāfirīn, 181, 187ff.; al-Bukhārī, *Ṣaḥīḥ*, Da'wāt, 15.

[64] Cf. Qur'ān 7:151.

during this, you hear the call to ritual prayer (*adhān*), stop that which you are doing and devote yourself to making the responses to the man who makes the call to ritual prayer (*al-mu'dhdhin*). Thus when the man says *Allāh akbar, Allāh akbar* (God is the greatest, God is the greatest), you repeat it. Similarly, you repeat his every other sentence, except *ḥayy 'alā aṣ-ṣalā* (come to ritual prayer) and *ḥayy 'alā al-falāḥ* (come to prosperity); in these two cases you say 'there is no ability or power except with God, the All-high, the All-great' (*la ḥawla wa lā quwwata illā bi-Allāhi al-'aliyyi al-'aẓīm*). When he says *aṣ-ṣalātu khayrun min an-nawm* (ritual prayer is better than sleep), you say, 'you have spoken truly and you are right, and I bear witness to that (*ṣadaqta wu bararta, wa anā 'alā dhālika min ash-shāhidīn*). When you hear the call to the actual start of the ritual prayer (*al-iqāma*), you repeat that which the caller says, except his sentence *qad qāmat aṣ-ṣalā* (the ritual prayer has started); in this case you say, 'may God cause this ritual prayer to be established and to continue as long as the heavens and the earth continue to exist' (*aqāmahā Allāhu wa adāmaha, mā dāmati as-samāwātu wa l-ardu*).

When you have completed the responses to the man who makes the call to ritual prayer, supplicate:

> God, I beseech You, at the time of ritual prayer for You, of call to You, and of the retreat of Your night, and of coming of Your day, that You would bestow on Muḥammad Your favour of his being a means (*al-wasīla*) [65] of excellence and of an exalted rank, and raise him to the praiseworthy station (*al-maqām al-maḥmūd*) which You have promised him, [66] O the Most Merciful of those who show mercy.
>
> (اللهم انــى اسألك عند حضور صلاتك واصوات دعـــاتك وادبار ليلك واقبال نهاركم ان تـــوءتــى محمدا الـــوسيلة والفضــيلة والدرجة الرفيعةم وابعثه المقام المحمود الذى وعدته يا أرحم الراحمين).

If you hear the call to ritual prayer while you are yourself engaged in the ritual prayer, complete your ritual prayer and, after salutation [to your right and left by which you withdraw from your ritual prayer], make responses to the caller in the usual manner.

When the Īmām (i.e. one who leads ritual prayer) starts the

[65] For a discussion of the concept of 'means' in Islam see Ibn Taymiyya, *at-Tawassul wa l-Wasīla*, Beirut, 1390/1970.

[66] Qur'ān 17:79.

obligatory part of the Dawn Prayer, do not be engaged in anything except to follow him in it; the details of this will be given to you in [the chapter] on how to perform ritual prayer and what are its rules.

When [11] you have completed the ritual prayer, supplicate:

> God, bless Muḥammad, and [all the members of] his family, and greet them. God, You are peace and from You peace comes and to You peace returns; so greet us, Lord, with peace, and admit us into Your house, the abode of peace [i.e. Paradise]. Blessed are You, O Lord of majesty and honour! Glory be to my Lord, the High, the All-high!
>
> There is no god but God alone; He has no partner; to Him belongs the kingdom and to Him belongs praise; He gives life and causes death, but himself is Ever Living Who never dies; in His hand lies all good, and He has the fullest power over everything.
>
> There is no god but God, the Lord of favours, bounty and good praise. There in no god but God; we do not worship anyone except Him, making our religion sincerely for Him, [67] even though the unbelievers dislike it.

(اللهم، صل على محمد وعلى ال محمد، وسلم. اللهم، انت السلام ومنك السلام واليك يعود السلام، فحينا ربنا بالسلام، وادخلنا دارك دارالسلام، تباركت ياذاالجلال والاكرام. سبحان ربى العلى الاعلى. لا اله الا الله وحده، لاشريك له، له الملك وله‌الحمد، يحيى ويميت وهو حى لايموت، بيده الخير، وهو على كل شيء قدير. لااله الا الله اهل‌النعم والفضل والثناء الحسن. لا اله الا الله، ولانعبد الا اياه مخلصين له الدين، ولو كره الكافرون.)

After this, supplicate to God by reciting that comprehensive and perfect supplication which the Messenger of God (may God bless him and greet him!) taught to ‘Ā’isha [68] (may God be pleased with her!). So supplicate:

> God, surely I beseech You to grant me all forms of good in this life and the next, both those which I know and those

[67] Qur’ān 40:17. Worship of God with sincerity is stressed in at least twenty-two verses of the Qur’ān.

[68] ‘Ā’isha binti Abī Bakr aṣ-Ṣiddīq (d. 58/678) was a favourite wife of the Prophet. She has the title of ‘mother of the believers’ (Qur’ān 33:6). She was a prolific narrator of Tradition and a model of piety. For an account of her see W.Montgomery Watt, “Ā’isha”, *EI*[2], I, 307f.

which I do not know; I seek the protection of You from all forms of evil in this life and the next, both those which I know and those which I do not.

I beseech You to grant me Paradise and every word and deed, every intention and belief which will bring me near to it; I seek the protection of You from Hell and from every word and deed, every intention and belief, which will bring me near to it.

I beseech You to grant me the good for which Your servant and Messenger, Muḥammad, (may God bless him and greet him!) prayed to You; I seek the protection of You from the evil from which Your servant and Messenger, Muḥammad, (may God bless him and greet him!) sought Your protection. God, make the outcome of whatever You have ordained for me good and right.

(اللهمّ انى أسألك من الخير كله عاجله واجله ما علمت منه
ومالم أعلم‌ وأعوذبك من الشر كله عاجله واجله ما علمت منه
ومالم أعلم. وأسألك الجنة وما يقرب اليها من قول وعمل
ونية واعتقادٍ واعوذ بك من النار ومايقرب اليها من قول
وعمل ونية واعتقاد. وأسألك من خير ماسألك منه عبدك
ورسولك محمد صلى الله عليه وسلمٍ وأعوذ بك من شرما
استعاذك منه عبدك ورسولك محمد صلى الله عليه وسلم.
اللهمّ وما قضيت لى من امر فاجعل عاقبته رشدا).

After this, supplicate by reciting that supplication which the Messenger of God (may God bless him and greet him!) prescribed to [his daughter] Fāṭima [69] (may God be pleased with her!). So supplicate:

O the Ever Living, O the Self-subsisting and All-sustaining, O the Lord of majesty and honour, there is no God except You; it is for Your mercy that I appeal to You, and it is from Your punishment that I seek Your protection; do not leave me to my own care one moment, but make my every condition upright as You did for the righteous.

(ياحى يا قيوم يا ذاالجلال والاكرام‌ لا اله الا انت‌ برحمتك
استغيث ومن عذابك استجير. لاتكلنى الى نفسى طرفة عين‌
واصلح لى شانى كله بما أصلحت به الصالحين)

---

[69] For her biography see Ibn Ḥajar al-ʿAsqalānī, *al-Iṣāba*, IV, 365-68; Ibn ʿAbd al-Barr, *op. cit.*, 362-69.

Then supplicate by reciting the prayer of Jesus Christ (may the blessing of God and His greeting be upon both our prophet and him!). So supplicate:

> God, in this morning I am unable to repel that which I dislike and to gain that for which I hope. This morning has come through Your power and not through the power of any one other than You. In this morning I am obliged to perform my action. So no needy man is in greater need than I am of You, while no rich man is less in need than You are of me
>
> God, do not cause my enemy to rejoice over me, do not cause my friend to do evil to me, do not bring misfortune to my religious affairs, do not make this world the greatest of my cares or the sum of my knowledge, and do not empower over me for my sin any one who will have no mercy for me.

(اللهم، انى أصبحت لا استطيع دفع ما اكره، ولااملك نفع ما أرجو. واصبح الامر بيدك لابيد غيرك. واصبحت مرتهنا بعملى فلا فقير افقر مني اليك ولا غنى اغنى منك عنى. اللهم، لاتشمت بى عدوى ولا تسوء بى صديقى ولاتجعل مصيبتى فى دينى، ولاتجعل الدنيا اكبر همى ولا مبلغ علمى، ولاتسلط على بذنبى من لا يرحمنى)

Then supplicate by reciting any of the well known supplications which come to your mind. For this purpose memorize them from the supplications we have set forth in the Book of Supplications from the 'books' of our work, *The Revival of the Religious Sciences*. [70]

Your time between the Dawn Prayer and the rising of the sun should be allotted to four tasks. 1. Recitation of supplications to God (*da'wāt*). 2. Various forms of praise of God (*adhkār*) and glorification of Him (*tasbīḥāt*), and repetition of them with a rosary. 3. Reading of the Qur'ān. 4. Meditation.

Meditate on your own sins and misdeeds, your shortcomings in the acts of devotion directed towards your Master, and how you have exposed yourself to His painful punishment and great wrath.

[As part of your meditation] order your time, arranging your preoccupation [12] for the whole day, so that thereby you may be able to make good for any shortcoming which has preceded. Beware

[70] This is the ninth 'book' of the first part of *The Revival* and consists of thirty-six large pages in Arabic. Some of the essential teachings of this 'book' is to be found in Quasem, *Ethics*, pp. 194-99, 204-207.

of exposing yourself during that day to the dire wrath of God. Make the intention of doing good to all Muslims. Resolve that throughout the day you will occupy yourself only with obeying God (exalted is He!). Go over in your mind all the different acts of obedience within your power, choose the noblest of them, and consider the means of it so that you may be occupied with it.

Do not omit reflection on the approach of your appointed term [i.e. the time of death] and the coming of death, which will cut short all your worldly hopes and as a result of which the whole matter will go out of your control and you will experience regret, remorse and long-drawn-out delusion.

In your various forms of glorification of God and praise of Him [before sun-rise], the following ten sentences should be included.

> There is no god but God alone; He has no partner; to Him belongs the kingdom and to him belongs praise; He gives life and causes death, but Himself is Ever Living Who does not die; in His hand is all good; He has the fullest power over everything. [71]

(لا اله الا الله وحده لاشريك له الملك وله الحمد يحيى ويميت وهو حى لايموت بيده الخير وهو على كل شىء قدير).

There is no god but God, the True and Manifest King. [72]

(لا اله الا الله الملك الحق المبين)

There is no god but God alone, the All-subduer, the Lord of the heavens and the earth and whatever is between the two, the Mighty, the All-forgiver.

(لا اله الا الله الواحد القهار رب السموات والارض وما بينهما العزيز الغفار)

Glory be to God!; praise be to God!; there is no god but God; God is the greatest; there is no ability or power except with God, the High, the Great.

(سبحان الله والحمد لله ولا اله الا الله والله أكبر ولاحول ولاقوة الا بالله العلى العظيم)

He is Most Glorified, Most Sanctified, Lord of the angels and the Spirit.

(سبوح قدوس رب الملائكة والروح)

---

[71] Qur'ān 9:116, 25:2, 57:2, 64:1. [72] Cf. Qur'ān 20:114, 23:116.

Glory be to God and praise be to Him!; praise be to God, the Great!

(سبحان الله وبحمده سبحان الله العظيم)

I seek forgiveness from God, the Great, save Whom there is no god, the Ever Living, the Self-subsisting and All-sustaining; I beseech You for repentance and forgiveness.

(استغفر الله العظيم الذى لا اله الا هو الحى القيوم، وأسأله التوبة والمغفرة)

God, there is no one who can withhold that which You bestow, and there is no one who can bestow that which You withhold; there is no one who can oppose that which You have ordained; good fortune cannot benefit its possessor apart from You.

(اللهم، لا مانع لما اعطيت، ولا معطى لما منعت، ولاراد لما قضيت، ولاينفع ذاالجد منك الجد)

God, bless Muḥammad and his family and his companions, and greet them all.

(اللهم، صل على محمد وعلى ال محمد وصحبه، وسلم)

In the name of God along with Whose name nothing can harm whether in the earth or in the heaven; He is the All-hearing, the All-knowing.

(بسم الله الذى لايضر مع اسمه شىء فى الارض ولا فى السماء، وهوالسميع العليم)

Repeat each of these sentences a hundred times or seventy times or ten times; the last is the lowest number which make the total a hundred. Continue these ten forms of praise of God, and do not speak before the rising of the sun. There is a Tradition that the recitation of these ten sentences until sun-rise uninterrupted by conversation is more excellent than the emancipation of eight slaves from the descendants of the prophet Ishmael (may God's blessing and greeting be upon both our prophet and him!).

MOST EXCELLENT PROCESSES OF PASSING THE TIME

[No ritual prayer can be performed from after the Dawn Prayer to the time when the sun is up. From this time to sun-declining there are two supererogatory ritual prayers the rewards of which are very

great. The time left over them should be spent by a very pious Muslim in any of four ways mentioned in this chapter.]

When the sun has risen and is a spear's length up, perform two [sunna] *rak'as* of ritual prayer, and this should be after the time disliked by God (*makrūh*) for ritual prayer — because ritual prayer is disliked by God between the time of performing the two obligatory *rak'as* of the Dawn Prayer and the time when the sun is up.

Then when the sun is high and about a quarter of the day has elapsed, perform the Forenoon Prayer (*Ṣalāt aḍ-Ḍuḥā*), four or six or eight *rak'as* in pairs. [13] All these numbers are related from the Messenger of God (may God bless him and greet him!). Ritual prayer of any number of *rak'as* is good; if a man wants, let him perform a large number of *rak'as* and if he wants, let him perform a small number. Between sunrise and the time when the sun begins to decline, there is no sunna ritual prayer except these two ritual prayers [just mentioned]. The time which is left over, you can spend in four ways.

1. The best way is to spend this time seeking really useful knowledge, not the superfluities with which people busy themselves and which they call knowledge. [73] Really useful knowledge is that which increases your fear of God, your insight into your own faults, and your knowledge of acts of devotion to God; it decreases your desire for the world, and increases your desire for the Hereafter; it opens your insight into the defects of your actions so that you guard against them, and makes you aware of the wiles and deceptions of Satan and how he confuses the evil religious scholars until he exposes them to the hate and wrath of God (exalted is He!); they buy this world at the price of religion and make their knowledge a means of gaining wealth from the oppressive rulers and of [unjustly] eating up the wealth of trust-endowments [for religious institutions], of the orphans [74] and the poor; all their thoughts throughout the day

---

[73] The ṣūfīs distinguish between useful knowledge and useless knowledge, and in this they are influenced by a Tradition that the Prophet used to seek protection with God from knowledge that is not useful. For this Tradition see *supra*, p. 20.

[74] Cf. Qur'ān 6:152, 17:37, 4:2, 4:17 where unjustly eating up the wealth of orphans is strictly prohibited, and a severe punishment for it in the Hereafter is clearly stated. In many other verses, different kinds of misbehaviour to them are strongly condemned, and respect for, and help to, them in various forms are commanded. Concerning the reward of taking responsibility for an orphan, the Prophet said that in Paradise his own rank and that of one who takes the responsibility of an orphan will be as close as two fingers. See al-Bukhārī, *Ṣaḥīḥ*, Ṭalāq, 25, Adab, 24; Muslim, *Ṣaḥīḥ*, Zuhd, 42; at-Tirmidhī, *Sunan*, Birr, 14.

are directed to the quest of influence and high status in people's minds, and this forces them to ostentation, quarrel, discussion of subtle theological matters and boastfulness.

This concept of useful knowledge we have expounded in our book, *The Revival of the Religious Sciences.* [75] If you are fit for it, acquire it and act in accordance with it, and then teach it and call people to it. Whoever acquires this useful knowledge, acts in accordance with it, and then calls others to it, is called great in the kingdom of heaven, according to the witness of Jesus Christ (may peace be upon him!).

When you have completed the acquisition of really useful knowledge and have also completed the task of reforming yourself outwardly and inwardly, and you still have some free time, there is no harm in spending it in the study of the schools of Islamic jurisprudence in order to know the less common details with regard to the acts of devotion to God, and the method of mediation between men when the following of passions leads them into quarrel. This too comes after the completion of the important tasks [i.e. after the acquisition of really useful knowledge and reformation of yourself outwardly and inwardly], and is included in the 'collective obligation'. [76]

Should, because of its occupation with those tasks which are included in 'collective obligation', your carnal soul call upon you to abandon the recitation of parts of the Qur'ān (*awrād*) and the various forms of praise of God which we have cited above, know that the accursed Satan has secretly infected your soul with a latent disease which is love of influence and wealth. Take care not to be deceived by that and become a laughing-stock for Satan, who will cause you to be destroyed and then mock at you. If, however, you have tested your carnal soul for a time with acts of Qur'ān-reading, praise of God, and other forms of devotional acts, and have found that it does not consider these acts burdensome through sloth, and if, rather, it is clear that you long to acquire really useful knowledge with the intention of only seeing the countenance of God (exalted is He!) and [happiness in] the Home of the Hereafter, then this is

---

[75] *Revival*, I, 13-41.

[76] 'Collective obligation' is an obligation upon all members of the society. If, however, fulfilled by a single member, it is no longer the responsibility of all others. If it is fulfilled by no one, all members of the society become sinners. The opposite of 'collective obligation' is 'individual obligation' (*fard al-'ayan*) which is an obligation that must be fulfilled by every member of the society.

better than supererogatory devotional acts provided your intention is sound. The important thing is the soundness of intention. [77] If the intention is not sound it becomes a point where fools are deceived and men's feet slip.

2. The second [excellent] way [of passing the time between sunrise and the declining of the sun] is where you are unable [14] to acquire really useful knowledge, but devote yourself to various types of devotional acts, such as praise of God, Qur'ān-reading, different forms of glorification of God, and ritual prayer. This is the grade of the devotee and is the characteristic of the righteous. By this second way also you will be among those who will achieve success in the Hereafter.

3. The third excellent way [of passing the time between sunrise and the declining of the sun] is to busy yourself with activities which benefit Muslims and produce gladness in the minds of believers, or which facilitate righteous actions for the righteous, e.g. [a] service to Muslim jurists, to ṣūfīs. and to other religious people, and going about their errands; [b] exerting oneself in feeding the poor and the unfortunate; [c] going about, for example, visiting the sick and escorting funerals. All these activities are more excellent than supererogatory devotional acts, for these are acts of devotion to God and at the same time involve kindness to Muslims.

4. The fourth excellent way [of passing the time from sunrise to the declining of the sun] is that, if you are unable to perform the activities just mentioned, busy yourself acquring the necessities of life for yourself or for your family, in such a way that [a] no Muslim suffers any harm from you nor has anything to fear from your tongue or your hand, [78] and [b] that your religious nature has remained sound since you have not committed any sin. Should you do this, you will reach the grade of the people on the right (*aṣḥāb al-yamin*), even though you fail to ascend to the grade of high stages of those who are at the forefront (*as-sābiqūn*). This fourth way constitutes the lowest grade in the stages of religion; anything which is below this belongs to the fields of Satans. This 'anything' is that — I seek the protection of God from it — you busy yourself with any activity which will

[77] For a well known Tradition emphasizing the soundness of intention see al-Bukhārī, *Ṣaḥīḥ*, Bad' al-Waḥy, 1; Muslim, *Ṣaḥīḥ*, Imāra, 155.

[78] The Prophet said, "A good Muslim is one from whose tongue and hands other Muslims remain safe." See al-Bukhārī, *Ṣaḥīḥ*, Īmān, 4f., Riqāq, 26; Muslim, *Ṣaḥīḥ*, Īmān, 64f.; Abū Dāwūd, *Sunan*, Jihād, 2; at-Tirmidhī, *Sunan*, Qiyāma, 52, Īmān, 12; an-Nasā'ī, *Sunan*, Īmān, 8f., 11.

demolish your religious nature, or that you cause harm to any one of God's servants [i.e. human beings]. This is the grade of those who will be destroyed in the Hereafter (*al-hālikūn*). [79] So beware of belonging to this grade.

Know that in respect of his religion a man stands in one of three grades. [80] 1 He may be safe [from punishment of the Hereafter], namely, when he confines himself to the fulfilment of all obligatory duties and the avoidance of sins. 2. Or he may be 'above standard' (literally, 'making a profit'), namely, when of his own will, he does good works which draw man near to God, and supererogatory religious duties. 3. Or he may be below standard (literally, 'incurring a loss'), namely, when he falls short of that which is incumbent upon him. If you are unable to be 'above standard', at least strive hard to be one who will be safe. Beware, again, beware of being 'below standard'!

In respect of other men also, a man stands in one of three grades. [81] 1. With regard to them he may take the place of 'noble and just angels', [82] namely, by exerting himself for their ends through compassion and the desire to fill their minds with gladness. 2. Or with regard to other men he may occupy the position of animals and inanimate objects, namely, where they receive neither benefit nor harm from him. 3. Or with regard to them he may occupy the position of scorpions, snakes and harmful beasts of prey, from which men expect no good, while fearing the evil they may cause. If you are unable to reach the high grade of the angels, at least take care not to fall from the grade of the lower animals and inanimate objects to the rank of scorpions, snakes and beasts of prey. If you are content to come down from the highest of heights, at least do not be content to be hurled into the lowest of depths. Perhaps you will be saved [from the punishment of the Hereafter] by the middle way where you will have neither more nor less than what suffices.

Then throughout the day, you must busy yourself only with those matters which will benefit you in the next life or in the present life — matters which themselves are indispensable to you and the aid of which is indispensable to the affairs of your Hereafter or this life. If

[79] Al-Ghazālī's distinction between three grade of people mentioned here is based on Qur'ān 56:7-94, 74:39, 7:36-53. See Quasem, *Jewels*, p. 220.

[80] These three grades are briefly discussed in Quasem, *Ethics*, pp. 194-99.

[81] For a brief treatment of these three grades see *ibid.*, pp. 208-12.

[82] Qur'ān 80:16.

[15] in your association with your fellow-men, you are unable to fulfil your religious duties and feel insecure [from punishment of the Hereafter], it is better for you to adopt solitude: so you must adopt it, and find in it salvation and safety. If in solitude, evil suggestions [come to your mind and] draw you away to that which is not pleasing to God and you are unable to subdue them by devotional practices, then you must sleep. This is the best state for you and for us. For this is [as though] having been unable to gain any spoils of battle we at least save ourselves by flight. But how lowly is the state of a man who saves his religious nature by making his life without work! sleep is brother of death, and renders life without work and joins it with inanimate objects.

THE BEST METHODS OF PREPARATION FOR RITUAL PRAYERS

[How a good Muslim should prepare for the Dawn Prayer and for the two supererogatory ritual prayers to be performed after sunrise is discussed in the preceding chapter. Preparation for all other ritual prayers following the most excellent methods is the subject-matter of the present chapter. The most profitable way of utilizing the time between every two ritual prayers is also suggested here. To a pious Muslim, time is very important — by making the best use of it, he can achieve happiness in his eternal life. So he orders his activities throughout the day and night having something fixed to occupy at every hour.]

You should prepare, before the sun begins to decline, for the Noon prayer (*Salāt az-Zuhur*). If you have the habit of rising at night for supererogatory ritual prayers, [especially the *Tahujjud* Prayer], or the habit of remaining awake at night for any other good purpose, then take your siesta (*qaylūla*) before midday; for it is an aid to night-rising, just as a meal immediately before dawn is an aid to fasting. A siesta, if you do not rise at night, is like a meal just before dawn when you are not fasting by day. Try to wake up from your siesta before the sun begins to decline.

After siesta, perform ablution, go to the mosque, perform [two *rak'as* of the] ritual prayer of greeting the mosque (*tahiyyat al-masjid*), and await the call to ritual prayer and [when this call is made] make the appropriate responses to it.

Then stand up and perform four *rak'as* following the decline of the sun. The Messenger of God (may God bless him and greet him!) used to lengthen them and to say,

> "This is the time in which the gates of heaven are opened, and I like that a good action of mine should be raised up to heaven at this time."

These four *rak'as* are emphasized sunna. Thus it is found in Tradition that

> whoever performs them, making the bowing (*rukū'*) and prostrating in the best way, is accompanied in his ritual prayer by seventy thousand angels, who continue to pray for his forgiveness until night.

Then perform the obligatory four *rak'as* of the Noon Prayer along with the Imām [i.e. the man who leads the ritual prayer]. After this perform two *rak'as* which belong to the established sunna prayer.

From this time until the Late-afternoon Prayer (*Ṣalāt al-'Aṣr*) do not be occupied with anything except the acquisition of knowledge, or assistance to a Muslim, or Qur'ān-reading, or effort in procuring such necessities of life as will be of assistance to you in your religious affairs.

Then when the time of the Late-afternoon Prayer is come, perform four *rak'as* before the obligatory *rak'as* of this ritual prayer. These four *rak'as* are emphasized sunna. Indeed, the Messenger of God (may God bless him and greet him!) prayed:

> "May God bestow His mercy upon a man who performs four *rak'as* before the [obligatory *rak'as* of] the Late-afternoon Prayer." [83]

So make an effort to receive the mercy of God for which the Prophet (may God bless him and greet him!) prayed.

After the Late-afternoon Prayer until the sun-set, occupy yourself only with the activities similar to those which are recommended above to be done after the Noon Prayer. You should not waste your time, doing at each hour only that which you happen to do by chance. Rather you should keep a strict reckoning with yourself and order your duties and activities throughout the day and night, having something fixed to occupy every hour, and neither doing anything outside its fixed time nor doing anything else in that time. It is in this way that the blessing of your time will be evident. If, however, you are aimless and neglect yourself, as the lower animals do, so that you do not know with what activity you have to be

---

[83] At-Tirmidhī, *Sunan*, Ṣalā, 201; Ibn Ḥanbal, *Musnad*, II, 117.

occupied each hour, most of your time will pass in waste [16] and your life will have slipped from you. Your life is your capital or the basis of your trading; by it you have to attain to the delight of the Eternal Abode [i.e. Paradise] in the near presence of God (exalted is He!). Every breath you draw is a jewel of inestimable worth, for nothing can replace it. Once it has passed, it cannot come back.

Do not, therefore, be like the deluded fools who delight every day at the increase of their wealth with the decrease of their days. What good is there in increase of wealth while life is decreasing? Delight only in the increase of knowledge and good action, for certainly these two are your companions that will continue to live with you in the grave, when your family, your wealth, your children, and your friends are all left behind. [84]

When the sun becomes yellow, try, before it sets, to return to the mosque, and occupy yourself with glorification of God and prayer for forgiveness of sins. The excellence of this time is like that of the time before sunrise. God has commanded,

> "Glorify your Lord with His praise before the rising of the sun and before its setting." [85]

(وسبح بحمد ربك قبل طلوع الشمس و قبل غروبها)

Before the sun sets, recite [1] the Qur'ānic sūra which begin with the verse, "We call to witness the sun and its growing brightness," [86] [2] the sūra beginning with the verse, "We call to witness the night when it covers up," [87] and [3] the two sūras by which one seeks the protection of God. [88] Let the sun set while you are still in prayer for forgiveness.

When you have heard the call (adhān) to the Sunset Prayer, make the responses to it and after this supplicate:

> God, at the approach of Your night and the withdrawal of

[84] Knowledge and action are the only two things that will be useful in the Hereafter. It is these two, says al-Ghazālī, which are meant in the Qur'ānic verse 18:46. For an elaborate discussion of knowledge and action as the two means of happiness in the Hereafter see Quasem *Ethics*, pp. 58-78, espicially, 64-78.

[85] Qur'ān 20:130.

[86] This is the ninety-first sūra of the Qur'ān consisting of fifteen short verses. It is entitled The Sun (*ash-Shams*).

[87] This is the ninety-second sūra of the Qur'ān entitled The Night (*al-Layl*). It consists of twenty-one short verses.

[88] Qur'ānic suras 113 and 114, consisting of five and six short verses respectively. They are entitled Daybreak (*al-Falaq*) and Men (*an-Nās*) respectively.

Your day, at the time of ritual prayer for You and of the voices of those who are calling to You [i.e. voice of *mu'adhdhin* at various mosques], I pray to You to bestow upon Muḥammad the favour of being a means [89] to rescue the believers from Hell, of excellence, nobility and an exalted rank, and to raise him to the praiseworthy station You have promised him; [90] surely You do not break Your promise.

(اللهم انى اسئلك عند اقبال ليلك، وادبار نهارك، وحضور صلاتك، واصوات دعاتك ان توءتى محمداالوسيلة والفضيلة والشرف والدرجة الرفيعة، وابعثه المقام المحمود الذى وعدته. انك لا تخلف الميعاد)

This supplication is like the one already cited.

Then, after making the responses to the *mu'adhdhin* as well as to the call for the actual start of the Sunset Prayer (*iqāma*), perform the obligatory *rak'as* of this prayer. After these *rak'as* perform two *rak'as* before speaking; these two *rak'as* are the fixed sunna of the Sunset Prayer. If you perform four more *rak'as* after these two *rak'as*, that is also a sunna.

After this, make, if possible, the intention of *i'tikāf* (seclusion for complete devotion) in the mosque until the Evening Prayer (*Ṣalāt al-'Ishā'*) and perform a supererogatory ritual prayer between the Sunset Prayer and the Evening Prayer. Concerning the inestimable merit of this supererogatory ritual prayer, much has come to us [in the Qur'ān and Tradition]. To this ritual prayer is the reference of the Qur'ānic verse starting with "Getting up at the beginning of the night for worship ...," [91] since this ritual prayer is the first act of worship that occurs at night. This is the Contrites' Ritual Prayer (*Ṣalāt al-Awwābīn*). Someone asked the Messenger of God (may God bless him and greet him!) concerning the meaning of the Qur'ānic verse, "The believers withdraw themselves from their beds." [92] He replied, "This verse refers to

> the ritual prayer performed between the Sunset Prayer and the Evening Prayer; it removes all idle words uttered from the beginning of the day to its end."

When the time of the Evening Prayer is come, perform four *rak'as* before the obligatory *rak'as* of this ritual prayer, thus filling the time between the call to this ritual prayer and the call to the actual start

[89] Qur'ān 5:35.   [90] Qur'ān 17:79.   [91] Qur'ān 73:6.   [92] Qur'ān 32:18.

of it. There is great merit in this. It is stated in Tradition that

> prayer between the call to ritual prayer and the call to the actual start of it is not rejected. [93]

Then perform the obligatory *rak'as*, and after this perform the two fixed sunna *rak'as*, reading in them the sūras entitled *Alif Lām Mīm as-Sajda* , [94] and the sūra beginning with the verse, "Blessed is He in Whose hand is the kingdom," [95] or the Sūra of Yā Sīn [96] and the Sura of Smoke. [97] This was the practice of the Messenger of God (may God bless him and greet him!). These two *rak'as* should be followed by four more sunna *rak'as*, the great merit of which is evident from Tradition.

Then perform the Odd Prayer (*Ṣalāt al-Witr*) of three *rak'as* with either two salutations or one. The Messenger of God (may God bless him and greet him!) used to read in this ritual prayer the sūra beginning with the verse, "Glorify the name of Your Lord, the Most High," [98] the sūra beginning with the verse, "Proclaim: take notice, O you who disbelieve!," [99] the Sūra of Sincerity [100] and the two sūras by which one seeks the protection of God. [101] If you have resolved to be up at night for supererogatory ritual prayers, postpone the Odd Prayer, so that it may be your last ritual prayer for the night.

After this occupy yourself with intellectual discourse or the study of a book. Do not be occupied with amusement and sport; if you do this, it will constitute the end of all your activities before going to sleep, since activities are judged by the one which is performed at the end.

[93] At-Tirmidhī, *Sunan*, Ṣalā, 44, Da'wāt 128; Abū Dāwūd, *Sunan*, Ṣalā, 35, 37, Jihād, 39,; Ibn Ḥanbal, *Musnad*, III, 119, 155, 225, 254.

[94] The thirty-second sūra of the Qur'ān consisting of thirty verses. It is entitled Prostration (*as-Sajda*).

[95] The sixty-seventh Qur'ānic sura consisting of thirty verses.

[96] The thirty-sixth sūra of the Qur'ān consisting of eighty-three verses. The Prophet called it "the heart of the Qur'ān." See Ibn Ḥanbal, *Musnad*, V, 26.

[97] The forty-fourth Qur'ānic sura consisting of fifty-nine short verses.

[98] Sūra 87 consisting of nineteen short verses.

[99] Sūra 109. It consists of six short verses.

[100] Sūra 112 consisting of four short verses. The Prophet regarded it as equal to a third part of the Qur'ān in respect of value. See Muslam, *Ṣaḥīḥ*, Musāfirīn, 260; at-Tirmidhī, *Sunan*, Ḥajj, 95. The reason for this is discussed in Quasem, *Jewels*, pp. 79f.

[101] These are the last two sūras of the Qur'ān consisting of five and six verses respectively. They are together known as the *Mu'awwidhatān* (the sūras of taking refuge with God) and are incantations or protective formulae to ward off evil, especially demonic suggestions. The practice of taking refuge with God is commanded at various points in the Qur'ān.

GOOD MANNER OF SLEEPING

[On completing the duties of the day and night when a Muslim comes to sleep, he should follow a few rules which are very simple, easy and meaningful. Observance of these rules will make his sleep fully Islamic; disregard of them, however, is not a sin. After sleeping in the Islamic way, a Muslim should also follow Islamic methods. Then as he starts doing his duties of the day he must keep himself within the bounds of Islam. Continuance in this Islamic way of life, for the rest of one's life, may naturally be felt hard and burdensome, but al-Ghazālī here suggests certain methods which will facilitate this continuance.]

When you intend to go to sleep, lay out your bed pointing to the direction of the Ka'ba in Mecca, and sleep on your right side, the side on which the corpse reclines in the grave. Know that sleep is like a death and waking up like Resurrection. Perhaps God (exalted is He!) will take your soul this night; so be prepared to meet Him by being clean through the performance of ablution when you sleep. Have your will written and beneath your head. Sleep after repenting of your sins, seeking forgiveness from God and resolving not to return to your sins. Resolve to do good to all Muslims if God (exalted is He!) raises you up again. Remember that in the like manner you will lie in the grave, completely alone; nothing except your action, will be with you, and only the effort you have made for action will be rewarded to you. [102]

Do not try to induce [too much of] sleep with effort, i.e. by spreading out a soft and smooth bed, because sleep makes you without any work [which is bad], except when to be awake is unwholesome for you — in that case sleep preserves your religious nature. Know that night and day are twenty-four hours; the amount of sleep you take altogether, by night and day, should not be more than eight hours. It is enough, supposing you live for sixty years, that you lose twenty of these years or a third of your life.

As you go to bed make ready your tooth-stick and the things which you will need, after waking, for ablution or for washing the entire boday if necessary. Resolve to get up during the night for supererogatory ritual prayer or else to get up just before dawn for the Dawn Prayer. Two supererogatory *rak'as* in the middle of the night is one of the treasures of the righteous man. Try to multiply your treasures against the day of your poverty [i.e. the Day of Judgement]. The treasures of this world will be of no use when you are

[102] Qur'ān 53:40.

dead. As you are about to sleep supplicate:

Lord, in Your name I lay me down and in Your name I shall rise up; forgive my sins. God, keep me from Your punishment in the Day when You will raise Your servants [i.e. men].

God, in Your name I live and die. God, I seek the protection of You from the evil of every evil man and from the evil of 'every living creature which You hold completely in Your powers; surely my Lord stands along the straight path [to guide and protect the believers].' [103]

God, You are the first — before You there is nothing; You are the last — after You there is nothing; You are the manifest — above You there is nothing; You are the hidden — beyond You there is nothing. [104]

God, it is You Who have created my soul and it is You Who will bring it to death. To You belong its living and dying; if You cause it to die, forgive it, and if You cause it to live, preserve it [from sin] as You preserve Your righteous servants [18]. God I beseech You for pardon and health.

God, awaken me in the hour most pleasing to You and use me in the action most pleasing to You, so that You may bring me ever nearer to Yourself and remove me ever farther from Your anger. I pray to You and You grant, I seek forgiveness and You forgive, and I call You and You answer.

(باسمك ربى وضعت جنبى وباسمك ارفعه فاغفرلى ذنبى. اللهم قنى عذابك يوم تبعث عبادك. اللهم باسمك احيا واموت. اعوذبك اللهم من شر كل ذى شر ومن شر كل دابة انت اخذ بناصيتها ان ربى على صراط مستقيم. اللهم انت الاول فليس قبلك شىء وانت الاخر فليس بعدك شىء وانت الظاهر فليس فوقك شىء وانت الباطن فليس دونك شىء. اللهم انت خلقت نفسى وانت تتوفاها لك محياها ومماتها ان امتها فاغفر لها وان احييتها فاحفظها بما تحفظ به عبادك الصالحين. اللهم انى أسألك العفو والعافية. اللهم ايقظنى فى احب الساعات اليك واستعملنى بأحب الاعمال اليك حتى تقربنى اليك زلفى وتبعدنى عن سخطك

<hr>

[103] Qur'ān 11:56.

[104] Cf. Qur'ān 57:3 — "He [i.e. God] is the first and the last, and the manifest and the hidden; and He has the fullest power over everything."

بعدا. أسألك فتعطني، واستغفرك فتغفر لي، وأدعوك
فتستجيب لي)

Then read [1] the Verse of the Throne (*Āyat al-Kursī*), [104a] [2] verses beginning from "The Messenger has believed" to the end of the Sūra of the Cow, [105] [3] the Sūra of Sincerity, [4] the two sūras by which one seeks the protection of God, [5] and the sūra beginning with the verse, "Blessed is He in Whose hand is the kingdom." Let sleep come upon you while you are remembering God and are clean [by ablution]. Whoever does this, lifts up his spirit to the throne of God, and he is written down as performing ritual prayers until he wakes up.

When you wake up return to those activities which I have mentioned to you first of all [i.e. in the first chapter]. Continue in this routine for the rest of your life. If continuing thus is hard for you, [do the following]. [a] Be patient in the same way as a sick man is patient at the bitterness of cure, since he looks forward to recover his health. [b] Reflect upon the shortness of life. If you were to live, for example, to be a hundred even, that would be little compared with your residence in the abode of the Hereafter which is eternal. Consider how in the quest for this present world you endure hardship and humiliation for a month or year, for you hope that thereby you will have rest for twenty years, for example. How, then, do you not endure the hardship of continuing that routine for a few days [i.e. the remaining part of your present life], in the hope of having rest for all eternity?

[c] Do not cherish the hope of living a long life; if you have this hope, performance of good action [for the Hereafter] will be burdensome to you. Suppose that death is near and say to yourself: I shall endure the hardship today, perhaps I shall die tonight; I shall be patient tonight, perhaps I shall die tomorrow. For death does not come upon us at a specified time or in a specified way or at a specified age; it necessarily comes upon us suddenly, and so preparation for it is better than preparation for this world. You know that you remain here for only a small period of time — perhaps there remains only a single day of your allotted span of life, perhaps only a single breath. Imagine this in your mind every day and impose upon yourself patience in acts of devotion to God daily. If, with the belief that you have fifty years to live, you lay upon your carnal soul the obligation of patience in acts of devotion to God (exalted is He!), your carnal soul will run away from them and be

[104a] Qur'ān 2:255.   [105] Qur'ān 2:285-86.

difficult to handle. If you do what I suggest, you will rejoice at death unceasingly; but if you put off and are easy going, death will come to you when you do not reckon on it and you will sigh unceasingly. When morning comes and the night journey is over, people praise night travel; when death comes, comes to you the news of the Hereafter; 'you will most certainly know the news of it after a while.' [106]

In the preceding chapters we have given you guidance in regard to the arrangement of your day and night. Let us now explain to you how to perform ritual prayer and how to fast and the rules of both, and the rules of leading a ritual prayer, of ritual prayer in congregation and of the Friday Assembly Prayer.

HOW TO PERFORM RITUAL PRAYER

[*Certain specific bodily activities and mental states form a ritual prayer. Bodily acts follow a sequence. To a non-Muslim these acts may appear difficult to perform, but to a Muslim these are easy and full of meaning. Mental states are: the devotee's submissiveness and humility towards God, the presence of his mind, his understanding the meaning and significance of the things recited in ritual prayer, and so on.*]

[a] When you have completed [1] the cleanliness of your body, clothing and place of ritual prayer from physical impurity, as well as [2] the cleanliness by ablution, and [3] have covered [19] your private parts from navel to knee, set your face to the direction of the Ka'ba in Mecca standing upright, leaving some space between your feet so that they do not touch one another.

[b] Then read the Qur'ānic sūra which starts with the verse, "Proclaim: I seek the protection of the Lord of mankind," [107] as a protection against the accursed Satan. Make your mind attentive to God and free it from all worldly suggestions. Consider in front of Whom you stand and speak, and feel ashamed of addressing your Master with a mind inattentive to Him and filled with wordly suggestions and abominable desires.

Know that God (exalted is He!) is aware of your most secret thoughts and sees your mind. He accepts your ritual prayer only according to the measure of your submissiveness, humility and lowliness. Worship Him in your ritual prayer 'as if you see Him; even if you do not actually see Him, yet He sees you.' [108] If your mind is

[106] Qur'ān 38:88.

[107] Sūra 114 entitled Man (*an-Nās*) consisting of six short verses.

not attentive and your bodily members not at rest, this is because of
your defective knowledge of the majesty of God (exalted is He!).
Suppose that an upright man, one of the leading members of your
family, is watching you to learn the quality of your ritual prayer; at
that your mind will be attentive and your bodily members at rest.
Then turn to your carnal soul (*nafs*) and reproach it: are you not
ashamed before your Creator and Master?; when you imagined that
you were observed by a humble creature of His, who was able neither
to benefit you nor to harm you, the parts of your body were
submissive and your ritual prayer was good; yet, though you know
that He observes you, you do not humble yourself before His
greatness; is He (exalted is He!) less in your eyes than one of His
creatures?; how great is your rebellion and ignorance and how great
is your enmity to yourself! [109]

Cure the disease of your soul by making use of these devices, and
[after the cure] perhaps it will be attentive to your ritual prayer. This
cure is essential because you are credited only with that part of your
ritual prayer which you perform intelligently and attentively; for that
part which you perform with inattention and negligence you are in
dire need of seeking forgiveness and making atonement.

[c] When your mind has become attentive, do not omit the call to
the actual start of the ritual prayer (*iqāma*) even if you are alone. If
you expect other people to take part, make the call to ritual prayer
(*adhān*) first and then make the call to the actual start of the ritual
prayer.

[d] When you have performed this latter call, make the intention
of this ritual prayer [e.g. the Noon Prayer], saying in your mind:

I perform the obligatory Noon Prayer for God (exalted is
He!) (اودى فرض الظهر لله تعالى)

Let this intention be present in your mind when you say *Allāhu
akbar* (God is the greatest); do not let the intention pass from you
before you complete the saying of *Allāhu akbar* .

[e] In order to say this *Allāhu akbar* raise your hands, which up
till now have been hanging loosely, to the level of your shoulders.

---

[108] Al-Bukhārī, *Ṣaḥīḥ*, Īmān, 37; Muslim, *Ṣaḥīḥ*, Īmān, 1, 5-7.

[109] This kind of reproach of the carnal soul (*mu'ātabat an-nafs*) is characteristical-
ly ṣūfistic; it forms part of the mystical virtues of vigilance (*murāqaba*) and self-
examination (*muḥāsaba*). Some stress on it is, however, laid by Muslim philosophers,
such as Miskawayh and al-Kindī. See al-Ghazālī, *Iḥyā'*, IV, 393-422; Quasem.
Ethics, pp. 173-76, 192.

The hands should be open and the fingers stretched out, but without any effort on your part either to keep the fingers together or to keep them apart. Raise your hands so that your thumbs are opposite the lobes of your ears, and your palms opposite your shoulders. When they are at rest in this place say:

Allāhu akbar (God is the greatest) (الله اكبر)

Then drop your hands gently. In raising and dropping the hands do not push them forward and draw them back, and do not move them sideways to right or left.

When you have dropped the hands raise them afresh to your chest. Give honour to the right hand by placing it over the left. Stretch the fingers of the right hand along the left forearm so that they grasp [20] the left wrist.

[f] Then, after saying *Allāhu akbar*, say:

> God is indeed the greatest. All praise belongs to Him. Glorify Him morning and evening.
>
> (الله اكبر كبيراً والحمد لله كثيراً وسبحان الله بكرة واصيلا)

Then read the following two verses of the Qur'ān:

> "I have singlemindedly devoted the whole of my attention towards Him Who created the heavens and the earth, and I am not one of those who associate partners with God." [110]
>
> (وجهت وجهى للذى فطر السموات والارض حنيفاً وما أنا من المشركين)

Then say:

> I seek the protection of God against Satan, the rejected.
>
> (اعوذ بالله من الشيطان الرجيم)

Then read the Fātiḥa [i.e. the Opening Sūra of the Qur'ān] [111] with special attention to its double letters (*tashdīdāt*), and try to make a difference between your enunciation of the letter *ḍāḍ* and *ẓā* [when reading the words *al-maghḍūb* and *aḍ-ḍallīn*]. Say *āmīn* at the end of your recitation of the Fātiḥa, without making it continuous with your recitation of the last verse of the Fātiḥa, "Those who have not gone astray" (*ghayri al-maghḍūb 'alayhim wa lā ḍ-ḍallīn*).

In the two obligatory *rak'as* of the Dawn Prayer and in the first

[110] Qur'ān 6:79.

[111] Sūra 1 consisting of seven short verses. For its merits see Quasem, *Jewels*, pp. 66-74.

two *rak'as* of the obligatory *rak'as* of the Sunset Prayer and the Evening Prayer, recite the Fātiḥa or any other part of the Qur'ān so loudly that it can be audible to a man very close to you. If, however, you are behind the Imām [i.e. one who leads the ritual prayer] do not read the Qur'ān loudly. In that case say only *āmin* loudly.

After the Fātiḥa. In the Dawn Prayer recite one of the long sūras of the Qur'ān; in the Sunset Prayer read one of the short sūras; in the Noon Prayer, Late-afternoon Prayer and the Evening Prayer read one of the medium sūras, e.g. the sūra starting with the verse, "We call to witness the heavens having stars," [112] and those sūras which are near to it in length; when travelling, read in the Dawn Prayer the sūra starting with the verse, "Proclaim: take notice, O you who disbelieve!," [113] and the sūra starting with the verse, "Proclaim: He is God, the single." [114]

Do not go straight on from the sura [you read after the Fātiḥa] to the *takbīr* [i.e. *Allāhu akbar*] of bowing (*rukū'*), but make a break between them long enough to say 'glory be to God!' (*subḥāna Allāh*).

Throughout standing, keep your eyes down and restrict your gaze to the place of the ritual prayer. This will help your concentration of thought and the attention of your mind. Be careful not to turn to right or left in your ritual prayer.

[g] Then for 'bowing' say *Allāhu akbar* (God is the greatest), raise your hands in the same manner as has been described, and prolong your saying of *Allāhu akbar* until you 'bow' completely. Then place your palms on knees, with your fingers stretched out. Set your back, neck and head all in one line. Keep your elbows away from your sides — a woman, however, will not do this, but keep them close to her sides. In this state of 'bowing' say three times *subḥāna rabbi l-'aẓim* (glory be to my Lord, the Great!). To say this seven or ten times is good if you are performing your ritual prayer alone.

Then raise your hand until you stand upright and raise your hand while saying, *sami'a Allāhu li-man ḥamidah* (may God hear him who praises Him!). When you are standing straight, say: *rabbanā laka l-ḥamdu mil'a s-samāwāti wa mil'a l-arḍi wa mil'a mā shi'ta min shay'in ba'du* (Lord, to You belongs praise filling the heaven, the earth and wharever else You please).

If you are in the obligatory *rak'as* of the Dawn Prayer, read the *Qunūt* in the second of these *rak'as* when you have stood upright

---

[112] Sūra 85 entitled The Star (*al-Burūj*) consisting of twenty-two short verses.

[113] Sūra 109 entitled *al-Kāfirūn*. It consists of six short verses.

[114] Sūra 112. See *supra*, n. 100.

after the 'bowing'.

[h] Then prostrate yourself saying *Allāhu akbar* , but not raising the hands. First place your knees on the ground, then your hands, then your forehead uncovered; place your nose on the ground along with your forehead. Keep your elbows away from your sides and your stomach from your thighs — a woman, however, will not do this, but will keep her elbows and stomach close to her sides and thighs respectively. Place your hands on the ground opposite your shoulders, but do not lay your forearms on the ground. In this condition say *subḥāna rabbi l-a'lā* (glory be to my Lord, the Most High!) three times, or, if one is performing the ritual prayer alone, seven or ten times.

Then rise from the prostration saying *Allāhu akbar* until you set upright with your left foot under you, while your right foot is erect. Place your hands on your thighs with the fingers outstretched, and supplicate: *rabbi ghfirlī, wa rḥamnī, wa rzuqnī, wa hdinī, wa jbirnī, wa 'fīnī, wa 'fu 'annī* (Lord, forgive me, have mercy on me, provide for me, [21] guide me, restore me, preserve me and pardon me).

Then prostrate yourself a second time in the same way as the first. [Raising your head from this prostration], sit upright for a few seconds for taking rest, in every *rak'a* at the end of which you do not read the Witnessing (*tashahhud*).

From this sitting for rest, stand up placing your hands on the ground but not moving one foot forward as you rise. Begin to say *Allāhu akbar* towards the end of the sitting which you did for rest, and prolong it until you are half-way up to a standing position.

[i] Perform the second *rak'a* in the same way as you have performed the first, repeating *a'ūdhu bi-Allāhi mina shshayṭānir rajīmi* (I seek the protection of God against Satan, the rejected), in the beginning. [After doing all other things of this second *rak'a*], sit [at the end of it] for reading the first Witnessing. When reading the first Witnessing place the right hand on the right thigh with the fingers closed except the forefinger and thumb, which are left free. [In reading the Witnessing] when you say *illā Allāh* (except God), and not *lā ilāha* (there is no god), point with your right forefinger. Place your left hand on your left thigh with fingers ourstretched. In this Witnessing sit on your left foot, as you do between the two prostrations [of every *rak'a*].

In the last Witnessing, however, sit on your hip. Sit on your left hip, with your left foot going out from beneath you and your right foot erect. [In this state] read the last Witnessing to the end of which add the Blessing (*aṣ-ṣalāt*) on the Prophet (may God bless him and greet him!). [115]

After this Blessing read the well known supplication which has come down from the Prophet. [116] After completing this supplication, say twice — once each side — *as-salāmu 'alajkum wa raḥmatu Allāhi* (may peace and mercy of God be upon you!). When saying this, turn your face so that your cheek may be seen from your sides, make the intention of withdrawing from the ritual prayer, and the intention of invoking peace on the angels and the Muslims who are on your both sides.

This is the form taken by the ritual prayer performed by a person alone. [The form of ritual prayer performed in congregation will be discussed in the following chapter.]

The reward of a ritual prayer depends on submissiveness and humility of the devotee, presence of his mind at recitation of parts of the Qur'ān, and acts of praise of God with understanding their meaning and significance. Al-Ḥasan al-Baṣrī [117] (may God — exalted is He! — have mercy upon him!) said, "Every ritual prayer performed with absent-mindedness is more likely to cause punishment to the devotee than reward." The Prophet (may God bless him and greet him!) said,

> "A man performs ritual prayer, but not even a sixth or a tenth of it is recorded for him [by the angels because he lacks attention and understanding]. Only that measure of a man's ritual prayer is recorded for him which he understands. [118]

METHODS OF LEADING AND FOLLOWING A RITUAL PRAYER

[Islam has laid strong emphasis upon ritual prayer in congregation (ṣalā bi-l-jamā'a). Such a ritual prayer has twenty-seven times more reward than the ritual prayer one performs alone. The procedure of the former prayer is to some extent different from that of the latter

[115] Al-Ghazālī has cited this formula in his *al-Wajīz*, Cairo, 1317 A.H., p. 45.

[116] This formula of supplication together with its transliteration and English translation is cited in Quasem, *Salvation*, Chap., III, sec. xi.

[117] Al-Ḥasan al-Baṣrī (d. 728 A.D.), a Follower (*tābi'ī*), was a saint, a great ṣūfī, a real ascetic, a sincere preacher, and a famous theologian. His sayings are often quoted in literatures on various Islamic subjects. For an account of him see 'Abd ar-Ra'ūf al-Munāwī, *al-Kawākib ad-Durriyya*, Egypt, 1357/1938, I, 96-99.

[118] An-Nasā'ī, *Sunan*; Abū Dāwūd, *Sunan*, quoted in al-Ghazālī's *Iḥyā'*, I, 161.

as discussed in the preceding chapter. The details of how a man leads a ritual prayer in congregation and how the congregation follows him are given below.]

The Imām [i.e. one who leads a ritual prayer] should make the ritual prayer light. Anas[119](may God be pleased with him!) said,

> "Never behind anyone did I perform a ritual prayer that was so light [120] and yet so complete as the ritual prayer led by the Messenger of God (may God bless him and greet him!)." [121]

The Imām should not say *Allāhu akbar* (God is the greatest) until the man who calls to ritual prayer (*mu'adhdhin*) has completed the call to the actual start of the ritual prayer (*iqāma*), and until the rows of the people are straight.

At every, *Allāhu akbar* the Imām will raise his voice, but his follower will not raise his voice except to the extent that he himself can hear it.

The Imām will make the intention (*niyya*) of leading the ritual prayer so that he may gain the reward of the act of leading. Even if he does not make the intention the ritual prayer of the congregation will be valid, provided they make the intention of following him, and they will obtain the reward of ritual prayer in congregation.

Like a man performing a ritual prayer alone, the Imām will secretly [1] read the supplication for starting the ritual prayer and [2] seek the protection of God against Satan. He, however, should *loudly* read [22] the Fātiḥa [i.e. The Opening Sūra of the Qur'ān] and another sūra [or part of another sūra] in all two *rak'as* of the Dawn Prayer and the first two *rak'as* of the Sunset Prayer and the Evening Prayer. The same will be done by the man performing ritual prayer alone. The Imām will *loudly* say *āmīn* in the audible part of the ritual prayer, and likewise the follower, making his saying of *āmīn* coincide with that of the Imām, not come after it. The Imām will remain silent a little at the end of the Fātiḥa in order to recollect himself. In this silence the follower will recite the Fātiḥa in the

---

[119] Anas Ibn Mālik (d. 91 or 93 A.H.) was a famous companion of the Prophet and a prolific narrator of Tradition. He was a servant of the Prophet until the latter's death. For his biography see Ibn Ḥajar, al-'Asqalānī, *al-Iṣāba*, I, 84f.

[120] To make a ritual prayer light one may reduce the number of verses in it after the *Fātiḥa* and not read the formulae of glorification of God more than three times. In an effort to make it light, however, one must not make it imperfect by omitting any of its parts.

[121] Al-Bukhārī, *Ṣaḥīḥ*, Adhān, 65; Muslim, *Ṣaḥīḥ*, Ṣala, 190, 196.

audible part of the ritual prayer so that he may be able to listen to the Imām's reading [a sūra after the Fātiḥa]. The follower will not read any sūra [after the Fātiḥa even secretly] in the audible part of the ritual prayer, except if he cannot hear the voice of the Imām [who is reciting a sūra after Fātiḥa.]

At the bowing (*rukū'*) and the prostration the Imām will not say *subḥāna rabbī l-'aẓim* (glory be to my Lord, the Great!) and *subḥāna rabbī l-a'la* (glory be to my Lord, the Most High!) more than three times. At the first Witnessing he will not add anything after the words *Allāhumma ṣalli 'alā Muḥammad* (God, bless Muḥammad!). In the last two *rak'as* [or the last one *rak'a* of those ritual prayers which consist of more than two *rak'as*] the Imām will limit himself to the Fātiḥa. He will not make the ritual prayer long for his followers. His supplication after the last Witnessing will not be longer than his Witnessing together with his Blessing on the Messenger of God (may God bless him and great him!).

In saying *as-salāmu 'alaykum wa raḥmat Allāhi* (may peace and mercy of God be upon you!), the Imām will make the intention of peace for the congregation, while the congregation, in saying *as-salāmu 'alaykum wa raḥmatu Allāhi* , will make the intention of responding to him. After completing the salutation the Imām will wait a little and face the people. He will not look at them if there are women among his followers, so that they may depart first. No one of the congregation will stand up until the Imām stands. The Imām will go off either to the right or to the left, as he pleases, but to the right is preferable.

The Imām will not specify himself in the supplication at the *Qunūt* of the Dawn Prayer, e.g. he will not say *Allāhumma ihdinī* (God, guide *me*); rather be will say *Allāhumma ihdinā* (God, guide *us*); he will say this loudly, and the congregation will say *āmīn* . In the supplication of the *Qunūt* they will not raise their hands, since that is not to be found in Tradition. The followers will recite the remaining part of the *Qunūt* consisting of the words *innaka taqḍī wa lā yuqaḍā 'alayka* (You pass judgement, but no judgement is passed upon You).

The follower will not stand alone, but will enter the row of the followers, or else drag others to himself. He should not precede or synchronize with the Imām in his actions, but should be a little after him; he should not bend for the 'bowing' (*rukū'*) until the Imām has come to the limit of the 'bowing', and he should not bend for the prostration so long as the Imām's forehead has not touched the earth.

METHODS OF FRIDAY ASSEMBLY PRAYER

[The excellence of Friday is very great in Islam. [122] A Muslim should take special preparation for this day. He is urged upon the performance of various forms of devotional acts as well as acts directed towards his fellow-men. The most important of these acts is the Friday Assembly Prayer (Ṣalāt al-Jumuʻa). The methods of this ritual prayer as well as the other devotional acts to be performed on this day are discussed in this chapter. Al-Ghuzālī advises Muslims to devote this day of the week especially to the Hereafter.]

Know that Friday is the festival of those who believe in God and in Muḥammad as His Messenger. It is a noble day; God (glorified and powerful is He!) ordained it for the Muslim community. On Friday there is an hour the exact time of which is unknown; if any Muslim by chance happens to pray to God (exalted is He!) for anything in that hour, most certainly God grants his prayer. [123]

Prepare, then, for Friday from Thursday by cleansing of clothes, by glorifying God enormously and by praying for forgiveness of sins on Thursday evening, since this Thursday evening is an hour equal in excellence to the unknown hours of Friday. Produce in your mind the intention of fasting on Friday, but do fast on Saturday or Thursday as well, since there is prohibition [23] of fasting on Friday alone.

When the morning breaks, wash your entire body [The Prophet said,] "To wash the body on Friday is required of every adult." [124]

The word 'required' here means established, emphasized [in Islamic Sharīʻa (revealed law)]. Then array yourself in white clothes, for these are the most pleasing to God (exalted is He!), Use the best perfume you have. Cleanse your body thoroughly by shaving your head or cutting the hair of your head, cutting your nails, using the tooth-stick, and doing all other forms of cleanliness, as well as by using fragrant perfumes.

Then go early to the mosque, walking quietly and calmly. The Prophet (may God bless him and greet him!) said,

"Whoever goes [to the mosque for the Friday Assembly

---

[122] See aṭ-Ṭabarī, *Tārīkh al-Umam wa l-Mulūk*, I, 56, 23; al-Bukhārī, *Ṣaḥīḥ*, Jumuʻa, 4; Muslim, *Ṣaḥīḥ*, Jumuʻa, 17f.

[123] Al-Bukhārī, *Ṣaḥīḥ*, Jumuʻa, 37; Muslim, *Ṣaḥīḥ*, Jumuʻa 13; at-Tirmidhī, *Sunan*, Jumuʻa, 2.

[124] Al-Bukhārī, *Ṣaḥīḥ*, Jumuʻa, 6; Muslim, *Ṣaḥīḥ*, Jumuʻa, 7.

Prayer] at the first hour, it is as if he offered a camel to God. Whoever goes at the second hour, it is as if he offered a cow to God. Whoever goes at the third hour, it is as if he offered a ram to God. Whoever goes at the fourth hour, it is as if he offered a chicken to God. Whoever goes at the fifth hour, it is as if he offered an egg to God. When the Imām comes out [for addresing the congregation], the leaves are rolled up, the pens are raised, and the angels [who wrote down people's names on the leaves] assemble near the pulpit listening to the praise of God [uttered by the Imām]." [125]

It is said that men's nearness to God at the time of looking upon the glorious face of God (exalted is He!) [in Paradise] will be commensurate to their earliness of going to the mosque for the Friday Assembly Prayer.

When you have entered the mosque make for the first row. If the congregation has assembled, do not step between their necks and do not pass in front of them while they are praying. Place yourself near a wall or pillar so that people do not pass in front of you. Do not sit until you perform the ritual prayer of greeting the mosque (*tahiyyat al-masjid*). The best is to perform four *rak'as* of this ritual prayer of greeting in each of which you read the Sūra of Sincerity fifty times. It is found in prophetic tradition that whoever does this will not die until he has seen, or, in a variant reading, has been shown, his place in Paradise. Do not omit the ritual prayer of greeting even if the Imām is giving the address. It is a sunna [i.e. a practice of the Prophet] to read in these four *rak'as* the Sūra of Cattle, the Sūra of Cave, the Sūra of Ṭā Hā, and the Sūra of Yā Sīn. [126] If you are unable to read these long sūras, read the Sūra of Yā Sīn, the Sūra of Smoke, the Sūra of Alif Lām as-Sajda and the Sūra of the Kingdom. [127]

Do not omit the reading of these [last mentioned four] sūras in the night preceding Friday, for there is great merit in it. One who cannot do this well should read the Sūra of Sincerity many times and supplicate many times for blessing on the Messenger of God (may God bless him and greet him!), especially on Friday.

When the Imām comes out for addressing the congregation, do

[125] Al-Bukhārī, *Ṣaḥīḥ*, Jumu'a, 4; Muslim, *Ṣaḥīḥ*, Jumu'a, 10; an-Nasā'ī, *Sunan*, Jumu'a, 14.

[126] These are, respectively, the sixth, eighteenth, twentieth and thirty-sixth suras of the Qur'ān.

[127] These are, respectively, the Qur'ānic sūras 36, 44, 32, and 67.

not perform any sunna or supererogatory ritual prayer and do not speak, but occupy yourself first with responding to the man who is calling to the ritual prayer (*mu'adhdhin*), and then with listening to the address and with accepting his admonition. Do not speak at all during the address. It is found in Tradition that

> whoever says to his side man 'keep quiet' while the Imām is addressing the congregation, has spoken idly, and whoever speaks idly does not obtain the merit of the Friday Assembly Prayer. [128]

This is because in saying 'keep quiet' he has spoken. So one should prohibit another from speaking by a sign, not by a word.

Then follow the Imam in the manner already described. After you have finished the prayer and said *as-salāmu 'alaykum wa raḥmat Allāh* (may peace and mercy of God be upon you!), before speaking read the Fātiḥa, the Sūra of Sincerity, and the two sūras of seeking the protection of God, each seven times. This will keep you safe [24] from one Friday Assembly Prayer to another, and will be a protection for you against Satan. After this supplicate:

> O God, O rich, O praiseworthy, O the One Who creates from the beginning and then repeats the creation, O Ever Merciful, O Loving One, make me abound in that which is lawful, in Your sight, in obedience to You and in grace from You, so that I turn from that which is unlawful, from disobedience and from all other than You.

(اللهم يا غنى يا حميد يا مبدىء يا معيد رحيم ياودود اغننى بحلالك عن حرامك وبطاعتك عن معصيتك وبفضلك عمن سواك)

After the Friday Assembly Prayer perform two or four or six *rak'as* in pairs. All these three were practised by the Messenger of God (may God bless him and greet him!) in various circumstances.

Then, [if possible], remain in the mosque until the Sunset Prayer or the Late-afternoon Prayer. Watch carefully for the noble hour [described above], for it may occur in any part of the day and perhaps you will find it while you are at the state of submissiveness and humility towards God. In the mosque do not go to the circles of people nor the circles of story-tellers, but to the circle of profitable knowledge — the knowledge which increases your fear of God

---

[128] Al-Bukhārī, *Ṣaḥīḥ*, Jumu'a, 36; Muslim, *Ṣaḥīḥ*, Jumu'a, 12; Abū Dāwūd, *Sunan*, Salā, 203, 229; at-Tirmidhī, *Sunan*, Jumu'a, 16; an-Nas'ī, *Sunan*, Jumu'a, 22.

(exalted is He!) and decreases your desire for this world. Ignorance is better for you than all knowledge which does not draw you away from this world towards the next. Seek the protection of God against unprofitable knowledge.

Supplicate much at the rising, declining and setting of the sun of Friday, at the call to the actual start (*iqāma*) of the Friday Assembly Prayer, at the preacher's ascending of the pulpit, and at the moment of people's standing up for starting this ritual prayer; it is likely that the noble hours described above will be at one of these times.

Try on this day to give such alms as you can manage, even if it is little. [On this day] do all sorts of good deeds — supererogatory ritual prayer, fasting, alms-giving, Qur'ān-reading, praise of God, solitary devotion in the mosque (*i'tikāf*), and after the performance of one ritual prayer in the mosque waiting for another ritual prayer.

Make this one day of the week especially devoted to the acts which will ensure your happiness in the Hereafter. It may, then, be an atonement for the remaining days of the week.

RULES OF FASTING

[*Fasting in the month of Ramaḍān is one of the five pillars of Islam. It is obligatory on Muslims. Fasting on other great days of the year mentioned here is supererogatory and upgrades man in Paradise. Fasting usually means abstention from food, drink and sex, from dawn to sunset. Perfect fasting, however, is something more. A pious Muslim makes his fasting perfect; he knows the aim, meaning and significance of fasting. All this is the subject-matter of this chapter.*]

You should not restrict yourself to fasting in the month of Ramaḍān and thus omit the business of supererogatory devotional acts and of gaining the higher grades in Paradise, so that you will have regret when you will look at those who fast and see them in the very highest grades, as if you were looking at a very bright star far above you. [129]

The great days — Traditions [130] bear witness to their excellence and nobility and to the generous reward for fasting on them — are the day of 'Arafa [i.e. the ninth day of the lunar month Dhū'l-Ḥijja]

---

[129] There are many grades in Paradise. Differences between the lower and higher grades are very great (al-Bukhārī, *Ṣaḥīḥ*, Bad' al-Khalq, 8; Muslim, *Ṣaḥīḥ*, Janna, 11). There are different grades in Paradise because of different grades in the believers' faith (*īmān*) and good deeds.

[130] These Traditions are cited in al-Ghazālī's *Iḥyā'*, I, 237f.

for those not making the pilgrimage to Mecca, the day of 'Āshūrā' [i.e. the tenth of the lunar month Muḥarram], the first ten days of the month Dhū l-Ḥujja, and the first ten days of Muḥarram, Rajab and Sha'bān. Excellent also is the fasting of the Holy months of the lunar year, namely, Dhū'l-Qa'da, Dhū'l-Ḥijja, Muḥarram and Rajab; of these, one is by itself and three adjoining one another. These are the great days in the course of one year.

In the course of a month the great days of fasting are: the first, the midmost and the last, together with the white days, namely, the 13th, 14th [25] and 15th.

In the course of a week the great days of fasting are: Monday, Wednesday and Friday. The sins committed throughout the week are atoned for by fasting on Monday, Wednesday and Friday. The sins committed throughout a month are atoned for by fasting on the first, midmost and last days of the month, and the white days, [namely, the 13th, 14th and 15th]. The sins committed throughout the year are atoned for by fasting for the days and months mentioned above.

Do not imagine that fasting is merely abstention from food, drink and sexual intercourse. Indeed the Prophet (may God bless him and greet him!) said,

> "Many a man who fasts receives nothing from his fasting except hunger and thirst." [131]

Rather perfect fasting consists in restraining all the bodily members from that which God (exalted is He!) dislikes. You should guard the eye from looking at disliked things, the tongue from uttering that which does not concern you, the ear from listening to that which God has forbidden — for the hearer shares the guilt of the speaker in the case of backbiting. Exercise the same kind of restraint over all other bodily members as over the stomach and genitals.

It is mentioned in Tradition that five things make a man break his duty of fasting: lying, backbiting, slandering, looking at someone with lust, and the false oath. The Prophet (may God bless him and greet him!) said,

> "Fasting is certainly a protection; if one of you is fasting let him avoid loose talk, transgression of divine commandments, and folly; if anyone attacks him or rebukes him let him say, 'I am fasting'." [132]

[131] Ibn Māja, *Sunan*, Ṣiyām, 21.

Try to break your fast with that food the eating of which is lawful (*ḥalāl*) in Islam, and do not take an excessive amount, eating more than you normally eat at night because you are fasting by day. If you take the whole amount you usually take, there is no difference between eating it at one meal at night and eating it at two meals [one by day and one by night, as when a man is not fasting]. The aim in fasting is to annul your desire and to multiply your capacity for works of piety. If, when you break your fast, you have eaten food equal to that which you could not eat throughout the day, you have thereby made up for that food which you missed; so you derive no benefit from your fasting, while in addition you find your stomach oppressive [because of overeating]. There is no vessel more hateful to God than a stomach full of that food the eating of which is lawful in Islam. What, then, if the food which fills it is that the eating of which is forbidden (*ḥarām*)?

When you have known the deep meaning and significance of fasting, do fast as much as you can, for it is the foundation of acts of devotion (*'ibādāt*) and the key of good works by which a man is drawn near to God. The Prophet (may God bless him and greet him!) said,

> "God (exalted is He!) has said, 'Every good deed is rewarded by from ten to seven hundred times as much, [133] except fasting, for that is for Me and I Myself shall reward it.'" [134]

The Prophet (may God bless him and greet him!) also said,

> "By Him in Whose hand is my life, the smell of the mouth of one who fasts is more fragrant to God than the scent of musk. God (glorified and powerful is He!) says, 'Should one give up sexual desire, food and drink for My sake, then the fast is for Me, and I Myself shall reward it,'" [135]

The Prophet (may God bless him and greet him!) further said,

[132] Al-Bukhārī, *Saḥīḥ*, Sawm, 2, Tawḥīd, 35; Muslim, *Saḥīḥ*, Siyām, 161f., Abū Dāwūd. *Sunan*, Sawm, 25; at-Tirmidhī, *Sunan*, Jumu'a, 79, Sawm, 54, Īmān, 8; an-Nasā'ī, *Sunan*, Siyām, 42f.; Ibn Māja, *Sunan*, Siyām, 1, Fitan, 12, Zuhd, 22.

[133] Qur'ān 2:261, 6:160.

[134] Al-Bukhārī, *Saḥīḥ*. Sawm, 2; Muslim, *Saḥīḥ*, Siyām, 164f.; Ibn Māja, *Sunan*, Siyām, 1.

[135] Al-Bukhārī, *Saḥīḥ*, Sawm, 2, 9; Muslim, *Saḥīḥ*, Siyām, 162ff.; at-Tirmidhī, *Sunan*, Sawm, 54; an-Nasā'ī, *Sunan*, Siyām, 41ff.; Ibn Māja, *Sunan*, Siyām, 1; ad-Dārimī, *Sunan*, Sawm, 50; Ibn Ḥanbal, *Musnad*, I, 46, III *passim*, VI, 240.

"Paradise has a gate called the Rayyān; only those who fast will enter through it." [136]

This measure of explanation of devotional acts which constitute the beginning of guidance is sufficient for you. When you need to know concerning divine tax (*zakā*) and pilgrimage to Mecca (*hajj*) or to have a fuller explanation of ritual prayer and fasting, consult our disscussion of these subjects in our work, *The Revival of the Religious Sciences* [26]. [137]

[136] Al-Bukhārī, *Ṣaḥīḥ*, Sawm, 9; Muslim, *Ṣaḥīḥ*, Ṣiyām, 162, 164f.
[137] *Iḥyā'*, I, 125-272.

PART TWO

THE AVOIDANCE OF SINS

PREAMBLE

[Islam enjoins the performance of certain things and the avoidance of certain things. In the first category are included the acts of devotion, a brief description of which is given in the preceding chapters. The things that must he avoided are identical with sins. Sins are committed when carnal desires are followed, crossing the limit set by Islam, and the instruments by which they are committed are the seven members of a man's body. These members are in fact God's gifts to man; they are created so as to be used for good purposes; but by making wrong use of them he commits sins. All these members must be prevented from the commission of sins. The sins from which they are to be prevented and the methods by which this prevention can be achieved are discussed in this part of the book.]

Know that religion has two parts. One is the leaving undone of all that is forbidden, and the other is the performance of acts of devotion to God (*aṭ-ṭā'āt*). The leaving undone is more difficult, for the acts of devotion are within the capacity of every one, but the setting aside of desires is only within the capacity of the most devout. For this reason the Prophet (may God bless him and greet him!) said,

> "The best flight (*al-hijrā*) is flight from evil, and the best fighter (*al-mujāhid*) is he who fights his passions." [138]

Know that you disobey God [i.e. commit sins] only with the help of your body's members. [In reality] these are a gift to you from God and a trust committed to you. To seek help from the gift of God in disobeying Him is the highest degree of ingratitude; to betray the trust which God has committed to you is the highest degree of

---

[138] Al-Bukhārī, *Ṣaḥīḥ*, Īmān, 4, Riqāq, 26; Abū Dāwūd, *Sunan*, Witr, 2, 11f., Jihād, 2; an-Nasā'ī, *Sunan*, Īmān, 9; Ibn Māja, *Sunan*, Fitan, 2; Ibn Ḥanbal, Musnad, II, 163, 192.

impiety. Your limbs are your subjects; so consider how you rule over them. [The Prophet said],

> "Each of you is a ruler, and [on the Day of Judgement] each of you will be asked concerning his way of ruling." [139]

Know that all parts of your body will certainly bear witness against you in the courts of Resurrection, with voluble and sharp, i.e. eloquent, tongue, thereby disgracing you before all creatures. God (exalted is He!) said,

> "[Consider] the Day when their [i.e. people's] tongues, hands, and feet will bear witness against them as to that which they used to do." [140]

(يوم تشهد عليهم السنتهم وايديهم وأرجلهم بما كانوا يعملون)

God (exalted is He!) [also] said,

> "On the Day [of Judgement] We shall put a seal on their [i.e. people's] mouths, and their hands will speak to Us, and their feet will witness to their doings." [141]

(اليوم نختم على أفواههم وتكلمنا ايديهم وتشهد ارجلهم بما كانوا يكسبون)

Guard, then, your entire body, especially its seven parts, for Hell has seven gates 'to each of which is allotted a fixed portion of the people of Hell.' [142] For these gates are fixed for only those who disobey God [i.e. commit sins] with the help of these seven parts which are: the eyes, the ears, the tongue, the stomach, the genitals, the hands and the feet.

SINS OF THE BODY

GUARDING AGAINST SINS OF THE EYE

[The eye is created by God so that man may use it for certain good purposes. But he makes wrong use of it and thus commits sins. It has to be guarded against four sins.]

The eye has been created for you only in order that you may be guided by it in darkness, that you may be aided by it in respect of your needs, that by it you may see the wonders of the realm of the

---

[139] Al-Bukhārī, *Ṣaḥīḥ*, Jumu'a, 11, Janā'iz, 32, Waṣāya, 9, Nikāḥ, 81, 90, Aḥkām, 1; Muslim, *Ṣaḥīḥ*, Imāra, 20; Abū Dāwūd, *Sunan*, Imāra, 1, 13; at-Tirmidhī, *Sunan*, Jihād, 27.

[140] Qur'ān 24:24.   14 Qur'ān 36:65.   [142] Qur'ān 15:44.

earth and the heavens, and derive lessons from the signs [you see] in them.

Guard the eye against three or four things — from looking at women other than those whom it is unlawful for you to marry according to Islamic religious law; from looking lustfully at a beautiful form; from looking at a Muslim with a look of contempt; and from perceiving faults in a Muslim.

GUARDING AGAINST SINS OF THE EAR

[The real purposes of the creation of the ear are mentioned in this chapter. By using the ear for other purposes man commits sins and suffers from evil consequences. These sins and their evil results are described here.]

Guard the ear against listening to heresy or backbiting or obscenity or vain conversation or mention of men's evil deeds.

The ear has been created for you only in order that by it you may hear God's (exalted is He!) speech [i.e. the Qur'ān], the Traditions of God's Messenger (may God bless him and greet him!), and the wisdom of His saints; and that, by gaining knowledge thereby, you may obtain access to the eternal kingdom and everlasting delight [i.e. Paradise]. If you listen with your ear to anything that is disliked [by God], then that [ear] which was [created] for your benefit will bring you harm and that [ear] which was meant to be a means of your success [in the Hereafter] will become a means of your destruction. This is the highest degree of loss.

Do not imagine that sinfulness belongs only to the speaker and not to the hearer. [Rather the truth is that one who listens to any sinful speech or word, is a sinner like its speaker.] It is mentioned in a Tradition,

> "The man who listens [to backbiting] is certainly a partner of him who speaks [backbiting], and is a backbiter like him." [143]

[GUARDING THE TONGUE AGAINST LYING, BREAKING PROMISES, BACKBITING, DISPUTING, SELF-GLORIFICATION, CURSING, INVOKING EVIL TOWARDS OTHERS, AND JESTING]

[God has bestowed a special favour upon man by creating the tongue for him. It is created for several good purposes. The ungrateful man, however, misuses it and thus commits sins which lead him to

[143] This Tradition is narrated by aṭ-Ṭabrānī and considered weak by al-'Irāqī in *al-Mughnī*, on the margin of al-Ghazālī, *Iḥyā'*, III, 146.

destruction in this world and in the Hereafter. A Muslim should keep his tongue under firm control. He should guard it against eight sins which are dealt with in the eight sections of this chapter. Each of these sins is defined here clearly, the evil it causes is mentioned, and the methods for its removal are also suggested.]

The tongue is created for you in order that by it you may greatly praise God (exalted is He!) and recite His book [i.e. the Qur'ān], that you may direct [27] His creatures [i.e. men] to His path, and that you may express your religious and secular needs, the feeling of which is present in your mind. When you have used it for a purpose other than that for which it is created, you have shown ingratitude for this gift of God (exalted is He!).

The tongue is the part of you which has most power over you and over all other people. It is the wrongful utterances of the tongue which will throw men into Hell on their noses. Gain, therefore, mastery over it to the utmost of your ability, lest it throw you to the bottom of Hell. We find in Tradition,

> "Surely man speaks a word in order to make his companions laugh; for this he will be hurled into the pit of Hell for seventy years." [144]

A Muslim became a martyr in battle in the lifetime of God's Messenger (may God bless him and greet him!). Someone said, "May he enjoy Paradise!" The Prophet (may God bless him and greet him!) said,

> "How do you know [that he is in Paradise]? Perhaps he used to speak about things which did not concern him and was niggardly with that which gained him nothing." [145]

Guard, then, your tongue against eight things [:lying, breaking promises, disputing, self-glorification, cursing, invoking evil towards others, and mocking].

1. Lying

Keep your tongue from lying, whether in earnest or in jest. Do not accustom yourself to lying in jest, for it may lead you to lying in earnest.

Lying is among the sources of the major sins. Besides this, if you become known as a lier, your uprightness is lost, your statements are

[144] Ibn Ḥanbal, *Musnad*, II, 402.

[145] Al-Bukhāri, *Ṣaḥiḥ*, Īmān, 33; Abū Dāwūd, *Sunan*, Jihād, 133.

rejected, and people's eyes scorn you and hate you.

If you want to know the evil of lying in yourself, consider the lying of someone else and how you shun it, hate its doer and regard his statement as abominable. Do the same thing in the case of your other faults. for you do not understand the evil of your own faults from your own case, but from the case of someone else. That which you regard as abominable in others is necessarily regarded by them as abominable in you. Do not, therefore, be pleased with that in yourself.

2. Breaking Promises

Take care not to promise something and then fail to fulfil this promise. Your beneficence to people should rather be in action without any words [by the use of which you make promises]. If you are compelled to make a promise, take care not to break it, except when you are unable to fulfil it or from compulsion, because breaking a promise is one of the signs of hypocrisy (*nifāq*) and an evil character. Thus the Prophet (may peace he upon him!) said,

> "There are three things which, if they are found in a man, mean that he is a hypocrite (*munāfiq*), even though he fasts and performs ritual prayer. [They are:] when he relates something, he lies; when he makes a promise, he breaks it; and when he is given a trust, he betrays it." [146]

3. Backbiting

Guard the tongue from backbiting. Backbiting is more serious than thirty adulteries according to Islam; this is reported in Tradition. [147]

The meaning of backbiting is the mention of anything concerning a man which he would dislike, were he to hear it. [If you do this] you are a backbiter and an oppressor, even if what you say is true. [148]

Be careful to avoid the backbiting done by the ostentatious Qur'ān-reciters. You do this if you make others understand your

[146] Al-Bukhārī, *Ṣaḥīḥ*. Shahādāt, 28, Īmān, 24; Muslim, *Ṣaḥīḥ*, Īmān, 102, 107, 109; at-Tirmidhī. *Sunan*, Īmān, 14; an-Nasā'ī, *Sunan*, Īmān, 20. For more information on breaking promises see al-Ghazālī, *Iḥyā'*, III, 132f.

[147] This Tradition is narrated by Ibn Abī d-Dunyā. See 'Irāqī, *op. cit.*. III, 141.

[148] Some people wrongly believe that mentioning a man's fault which is *really* present in him is not backbiting. The consensus of the Muslim community (*ijmā'al-umma*) is that mentioning the fault which is really present is backbiting, and that mentioning a fault which is not really present is both backbiting and falsehood (*buhtān*). This view is based on the following Tradition. The Prophet once asked his

purpose [i.e. to mention the fault of some one] without clearly stating it. Thus you say, 'May God make him a better man! what he has done has harmed me and grieved me; let us pray to God to make both him and us better.' This combines two evil things. One is backbiting, for by this people can understand [the fault of the man of whom you are speaking]. The other is self-glorification and self-praise for one's own freedom from sin and for goodness. If your purpose in saying, 'May God make him better!', were to pray for him, pray for him in secret. If [28] you are [really] grieved for his sake, the sign of it is that you do not want to express his faults and to disgrace him; but in expressing your grief at his fault you manifestly backbite him.

To restrain yourself from backbiting, the statement of God (exalted is He!) is sufficient:

> "Do not backbite one another. Would any of you like to eat the flesh of his dead brother? Surely you would loath such an act." [149]

(ولا يغتب بعضكم بعضا. أيحب احدكم ان يأكل لحم اخيه ميتا؟ فكرهتموه)

God has likened you to one who eats the flesh of a dead man. How fitting that you should guard against backbiting!

There is one thing which, if you reflect on it, will prevent you from backbiting the Muslims. That is to examine yourself to see whether you have any outward or inward fault and whether you are committing any sin secretly or openly. When you have [done this and] known about the presence of any fault or sin in you, then do understand that the other man's inability to free himself from the fault which you attribute to him is like your inability, and his excuse is like your excuse. Just as you dislike your own disgrace and mention of your own faults [by others], so he dislikes these. If you conceal his faults, God will keep your defects hidden; but if you disclose his faults and thus disgrace him, God will give sharp tongues power over you to impair your reputation in this world, and

companions, "Do you know what is backbiting?" They replied, "God and His Messenger know best." He said, "Backbiting consists in your saying things about your brother [in respect of religion] which he dislikes." Someone asked, "Is it backbiting if what I mention is *really* present in my brother?" The Prophet replied, "If what you speak of is present in him you have engaged in backbiting; if it is not present in him you have told a lie." See Muslim, *Ṣaḥīḥ*, Birr, 70. For a discussion of this see al-Ghazālī, *Iḥyā'*, III, 143f.

[149] Qur'ān 49:12.

in the Hereafter on the Day of Resurrection God will disclose your faults in the presence of all creatures and thus will disgrace you. If, on examining your outward and inward aspects, you are not aware of any fault and imperfection in them, either religious or secular, then know that your ignorance of your own faults is the worst of all forms of stupidity, and [clearly] there is no fault greater than stupidity. Had God enforced His will for your good, He would have shown you your own faults. Your being pleased with yourself [imagining that you are free from faults] is the extreme of stupidity and ignorance. If, however, you are honest in your imagination, be grateful to God (exalted is He!) for this [freedom from sin] and do not corrupt it by rebuking people and ruining their honour, for these are among the greatest faults. [150]

4. Wrangling, Disputing, and Discussing Subtle Theological and Metaphysical Matters

Avoid wrangling, disputing and discussing with people very subtle theological and metaphysical matters. These involve injury to the other party, ascription of ignorance to him, and defamation of him. These also involve self-praise and self-glorification by showing superior intelligence and knowledge. Moreover, these disturb one's normal living, for when you contend with a fool he only annoys you, and when you contend with a forbearing man he hates you and feels rancour against you. The Prophet (may God bless him and greet him!) said,

> "If a man avoids disputing when he is in the wrong, God builds for him a house in the middle part of Paradise. If a man avoids disputing when he is in the right, God builds for him a house in the highest grade of Paradise." [151]

Satan should not deceive you by saying to you, 'Make the truth manifest and do not dissemble about it'. Satan is always trying to entice fools to evil presented in the guise of good. Do not become a laughing-stock for Satan and have him mock at you. Your act of making the truth manifest is good when there is someone who receives it from you. That is by way of admonition in private, not by way of disputation. Admonition has a distinctive quality and form and requires kindness. Otherwise it becomes disclosure of defects and putting someone in disgrace; it is more evil than good.

---

[150] For more information on backbiting see al-Ghazālī, *Iḥyā'*, III, 141-54.
[151] At-Tirmidhī, *Sunan*, Birr, 58; Abū Dāwūd, *Sunan*, Adab, 7.

Whoever has associated with the theologians and jurists of this age [152] has, in his nature, a dominating tendency towards wrangling and disputation, and finds it difficult to be silent, since evil scholars have given him the idea that wrangling and disputation are what constitute excellence, and that the ability to [29] demonstrate and discuss is that which deserves praise. Flee from them as you flee from a lion. Know that wrangling causes the hatred of God and man. [153]

5. Self-glorification

Restrain the tongue from self-glorification. God (exalted is He!) said,

> "Do not ascribe purity to yourselves; He knows best him who is truly righteous." [154]

Someone asked a wise man, "What is bad truthfulness?" He replied, "A man's praise of himself." So beware of forming the habit of doing that.

Know that self-glorification reduces your honour in the estimation of people and necessarily leads to God's hatred of you. If you want to know that your praise of yourself does not cause an increase in your honour in the estimation of others, consider [your reaction to] those who are equal to you in age and merit when they praise themselves for their excellence, influence and wealth — your mind refuses to acknowledge what they claim, your nature feels it burdensome, and you blame them for it when you have left them. Know that, when you glorify yourself, they also blame you in their minds while you are present, and, after you have left their company, express their opinion in words. [155]

6. Cursing

Beware of cursing anything which God (exalted is He!) has created, whether animal or food or man himself. Do not accuse any

[152] This refers to the age of al-Ghazālī, in which dispute, debate, and argumentation on subtle theological and juristic points became very usual, and this badly affected relationships among Muslims.

[153] For a more detailed discussion of wrangling and disputing see al-Ghazālī *Iḥyā'*, III, 116-20.

[154] Qur'ān 53:33.

[155] A fuller discussion of self-glorification is to be found in al-Ghazālī's *Iḥyā'*, III, 131, 336-78.

[156] This is discussed in al-Ghazālī's *Fayṣal at-Tafriqa bayna al-Islām wa az-Zanādiqa.*

of the people of *qibla* [i.e. Muslims] as a polytheist or infidel or hypocrite, [156] for the One Who is aware of the secret [beliefs of the mind] is God (exalted is He!); do not interfere between God (exalted is He!) and His servants.

Know that on the Day of Resurrection you will not be asked, 'Why did you not curse so-and-so? Why were you silent about him? Rather even if throughout your life you have never cursed Iblīs and never employed your tongue in mentioning him, you will not be asked concerning that on the Day of Resurrection; but if you have cursed any creature of God (exalted is He!), you will be asked to give an account of it. Never blame anything created by God. Indeed,

> the Prophet (may God bless him and greet him!) would never criticize bad food; rather if he wanted anything, he ate it; otherwise he left it alone. [157]

7. Invoking Evil towards Others

Guard your tongue against invoking evil towards any creature of God (exalted is He!) even although he has oppressed you; leave the matter of his oppressing you to God (exalted is He!). It is mentioned in Tradition.

> "The oppressed prays for the evil of the oppressor until he requites him. Then the oppressor becomes his creditor, and will make his demand on the Day of Resurrection."

Once a certain man said much against al-Ḥajjāj. [158]   One of the righteous ancestors [who was present there] remarked: "Just as God will take vengeance on al-Ḥajjāj for those whom he oppressed, so He will certainly take   vengeance for al-Ḥajjāj on those whose tongues attack him." [159]

8. Jesting, Ridiculing and Mocking

Guard your tongue against jesting, ridiculing and mocking

[157] Muslim, *Saḥīḥ*, Ashriba, 187f.; al-Bukhārī, *Ṣaḥīḥ*, Aṭ'ima, 21; Abū Dāwūd, *Sunan*, Aṭ'ima 14; at-Tirmidhī, *Sunan*, Birr, 84. For a more detailed account of cursing see al-Ghazālī, *Iḥyā'*, III, 123-26.

[158] Al-Ḥajjāj ibn Yūsuf ath-Thaqafī (d. 95 A.H.) was one of the most famous Umayyad governors. The method which made him famous was indeed notorious — extreme severity, atrocities, and bloodshed more than was necessary. He shed blood even in the Holy city of Mecca and bombarded the Holy Ka'ba and the pilgrims there. See Ibn Qutayba, *al-Ma'ārif*, Cairo, 1969, p. 548.

[159] Invoking evil towards others is discussed in great detail in al-Ghazālī's *Iḥyā'*, III, 121-26.

people, whether in earnest or in humour, for these will disturb you as water in a pool is disturbed by a stone, will reduce [people's] awe of you, will gradually cause your isolation from them and will hurt their minds. They are also the source of importunity, anger and estrangement, and implant rancour in people's minds.

Do not associate with anyone in jesting. If people try to associate with you in their jests, do not reply to them but turn away from them 'until they engage in some other discourse,' [160] and be one of 'those who, when they come upon anything vain, pass on with dignity.' [161]

These sins are the evil acts of the tongue. Nothing will assist you against them except solitude [for some time] and preservation of silence always [30] except when there is need to talk. Indeed, the most devout Abū Bakr [162] (may God be pleased with him!) used to place a stone in his mouth to prevent himself speaking without necessity; he used to point to his tongue and say, 'This is what has brought all troubles upon me.' Guard against the tongue, for it is the chief cause of your destruction in this world and the Here-after. [163]

GUARDING AGAINST THE SINS OF THE STOMACH

[Islam has made certain foods lawful to eat while others are unlawful. To look for that which is lawful is the duty of every Muslim, just as it is his duty to perform ritual prayers five times a day. To take forbidden food is the sin of the stomach against which every Muslim should guard. He should also guard against food concerning the lawfulness of which he has doubt and which he imagines, on some grounds, to be forbidden. There are certain methods which enable man to obtain the lawful and to avoid the unlawful. All this is the theme of this chapter.]

Guard the stomach from taking that which is forbidden by Islamic religious laws and also that concerning the lawfulness of which there is doubt. Endeavour to find that which is made lawful by Islam, and when you have found it try to take less than your fill of it. Satiety hardens the mind, impairs intelligence and weakens the

---

[160] Qur'ān 4:140. [161] Qur'ān 25:72.

[162] Abū Bakr aṣ-Ṣiddīq (d. 13 A.H.) was the greatest companion of the Prophet, his son-in-law, and his successor. His contribution to Islam is only next to that of the Prophet himself. See Ibn Ḥajar, *Tahdhīb at-Tahdhīb*, Hyderabad, India, 1325-27 A.H. V, 315-16.

[163] For a detailed discussion of all evil acts of the tongue see al-Ghazālī, *Iḥyā'*, III, 107-63.

memory; it causes the limbs to be so heavy that performance of devotional acts and acquisition of knowledge become difficult; it strengthens the carnal desires, and helps the hosts of Satan. Satiety arising from that which is lawful according to Islam is a source of all evil; what then of satiety of that which is unlawful?

To look for that which is lawful is a duty of every Muslim. Performance of devotional acts and acquisition of knowledge while eating that which is unlawful, are like building on dung. If you are content with a coarse shirt throughout the year and with two loaves of black bread in twenty-four hours, and give up the enjoyment of the best type of condiments, then you will never lack a sufficient quantity of that which is made lawful in Islam.

That which is made lawful in Islam is of many kinds. You are not required to be certain about the unknown inner nature of things; rather you are required to guard from that which you know to be made forbidden in Islam or that which you assume to be so on the basis of indications actually present and which by analogy imply unlawfulness.

As for the things which are known to be forbidden, they are obvious. But the things which are assumed to be so on the basis of a sign [are not obvious and need to be mentioned. They] are the property of the oppressive ruler and his deputies, and the property of those who only earn from mourning for the dead [164] or selling wine [165] or practising usury or the playing of flutes or other instruments of pleasure which is forbidden in Islam. If a man is such that you know for sure that the greater part of his property was acquired by forbidden means, then that part of his property which you accept, although it was possibly acquired by lawful means, should be considered as acquired by forbidden means, since it is more probable that this part of his wealth was acquired by forbidden means. Among the absolutely forbidden things is the consuming of any trust fund where it is done other than in accordance with the provision of the testator. Thus anything which a person not engaged in religious studies receives from the trust funds of the religious schools is forbidden. If a person has committed a sin invalidating his giving witness, that which he receives as a ṣūfī from a trust fund or other source is forbidden for him.

[164] In pre-Islamic Arabia, some people had adopted the profession of mourning for the dead on payment. Islam prohibited this practice and declared the property earned in this way as unlawful.

[165] To sell wine, like its drinking, is unlawful in Islam, and the money earned by selling it is also unlawful.

We have discussed the bases of the doubtful things, the lawful things and the forbidden things in a single 'book' [166] of our work, *The Revival of the Religious Sciences*. You must seek to study this 'book', for to know that which is lawful and to seek it are a duty of every Muslim just like the five ritual prayers.

GUARDING AGAINST SINS OF THE GENITALS

[*Sexual desire is created in man for the continuation of human species. It can be satisfied only with married wives and slave women. Outside these, sex is strictly forbidden in Islam and a major sin. How to keep away from this sin is suggested in this chapter.*]

Guard the genitals from everything which God (exalted is He!) has forbidden. Be like those concerning whom God (exalted is He!) said,

> "[Successful shall be the believers...] who safeguard their genitals — there is certainly no blame on them in satisfying their sexual desire with their wives and with those whom they own [i.e. slave women]." [167]

(والذين هم لفروجهم حافظون؛ الا على ازواجهم او ماملكت ايمانهم؛ فانهم غير ملومين)

You can guard your sex only by guarding your eyes from looking [at those women whom it is lawful for you to marry according to Islamic religious laws], by guarding your mind from thinking [about sex], by guarding your stomach from food [the lawfulness of] which is doubtful, and from satiety, since these things move the desire [for sex] and constitute its seed-bed. [168]

GUARDING AGAINST THE SINS OF THE HANDS

[*The Islamic view concerning the hands is that they, like other bodily members, are created by God for certain specific purposes related to the good of body and soul. An explanation of such purposes is to be found in al-Ghazālī's The Revival of the Religious Sciences. The use of the hands for these purposes amounts to the*

[166] This is the fourteenth 'book' of *The Revival* divided into seven long chapters. Like al-Ghazālī, al-Makkī also emphasized the seeking of only that which is lawful. He devoted a complete chapter of his *Qūt*, II, (pp. 582-604) to the discussion of this problem.

[167] Qur'ān 23:5-6.

[168] The desire for sexual activity is discussed in great detail in al-Ghazālī's *Iḥyā'*, III, 99-107.

*expression of gratitude to God for His gift of creating the hands.
Their misuse or leaving them unused where they should be used
means ingratitude to God. Misuse of the hands results in sins. On
the Day of Judgement when the sinners, having seen Hell-fire
nearby, plead to God not to punish them without sufficient evi-
dence, God will give power to the hands and the feet to speak out
concerning the sins their possessors committed through them in this
world. This is clearly stated in the Qur'ān.* [169] *Some of the misuses
of the hands are mentioned below with an admonition to guard them
against them.*]

Guard the hands from beating a Muslim, [170] from receiving
wealth which is acquired by forbidden means, form harming any
[31] creature, from betraying a trust or deposit, and from writing
words, the utterance of which is not made permissible by Islamic
religious laws. The pen is one of man's two tongues; so guard it from
the things from which you also guard the tongue.

GUARDING AGAINST SINS OF THE FEET

[*Man's feet are a grace of God to him. The graces of God must not
be used to do that which is forbidden by Him. The forbidden things
related to the feet are of varied types. The feet must be guarded
against them all. Not only the movements of the feet, but man's
capacity to move any of his body's members or to keep them still is a
grace of God. Therefore, the members should not be moved to do
anything which is disobedience to God.*]

Guard your feet from going to forbidden places and from using
them to go to an oppressive ruler. To go to oppressive rulers without
necessity or compulsion is a major sin, for it means humbling oneself
before them and honouring them in their sinfulness, whereas God
(exalted is He!) commanded us to keep away from such rulers when
He said,

> "Do not incline towards those who do wrong, lest Hell-fire
> should afflict you and then you will have no protectors apart
> from God, nor will you be helped." [171]

(ولا تركنوا الى الذين ظلموا فتمــسكم النار الاية)

If you turn to oppressive rulers, seeking their wealth, that is
something which is forbidden. Indeed the Prophet (may God bless
him and greet him!) said,

[169] Qur'ān 36:65.   [170] See *supra*, n, 78.   [171] Qur'ān 11:115.

> "When a man bows himself before an upright rich man, two-thirds of his religious quality goes away."

This is in the case of a rich man who is upright; what then, do you think, of a rich man who is an oppressor?

In general, the movement and stillness of the parts of your body are among the graces of God to you. So never move any of these members in disobedience to God (exalted is He!), but employ them in obeying Him.

[CONCLUSION]

Know that if you fall short of doing this, the evil consequences will come back upon yourself; if you are diligent [in acts of devotion to God], the good consequences of your diligence will come back to yourself. God is independent of you and your action. 'Assuredly 'everyone is pledged to that which he has practised.' [172] Beware of saying, 'God is Generous, Ever Merciful; He forgives the sins of the disobedient.' This is a true statement, but what is meant by it in this context is false, and the person who repeats it is to be dubbed a fool, according to the definition of the Messenger of God (may God bless him and greet him!) when he said,

> "The shrewd man is he who considers himself below the standard and works for that which is after death. The fool is the man who makes himself follow his passions and desires things contrary to the command of God." [173]

Know that your statement [that God is Generous and forgives sins] is like the following statement of a man who wants to be learned in religious sciences but spends his time in idleness: 'God is Generous, Ever Merciful, Able to fill my mind with some of that knowledge with which he filled the minds of His prophets and saints, without any effort on my part, any repetition [of what is taught by a teacher], and any notes [from it].' Your statement is also like that of a man who wants wealth, yet does not engage in cultivation of land or commerce or any other way of earning wealth, but remains without works and says 'God is Generous, Ever Merciful and "to Him belong the treasuries of the heavens and the earth;" [174] He is able to make me aware of some treasure which will make me independent of earning livelihood; He has in fact done that for some

[172] Qur'ān 74:41.

[173] At-Tirmidhī, *Sunan*, Qiyāma, 25; Ibn Māja, *Sunan*, Zuhd, 31; Ibn Ḥanbal, *Musnad*, IV, 124.   [174] Qur'ān 63:7.

people.'

When you hear the statements of the two men [just mentioned], you consider them as fools and mock them, even though their description of God's (exalted is He!) generosity and power is true and correct. In the same way, men of insight in religion laugh at you when you hope for God's forgiveness without making any effort for it. [Against this attitude of yours] God (exalted is He!) says,

"Man will have nothing but that for which he strives." [175]

(ليس للانسان الا ما سعى)

"Assuredly you will be requited with that which you used to do." [176]

(انما تجزون ما كنتم تعملون)

"Verily the pious will be in the delight [of Paradise], and the wicked in Hell." [177]

(ان الابرار لفى نعيم، وان الفجار لفى جحيم)

If you do not, while still relying on God's generosity, give up efforts to acquire knowledge and wealth you should likewise not give up making provision for the Hereafter and not become remiss. The Lord [32] of this world and of the next is one, and in both He is Generous and Merciful; His generosity does not increase through your acts of obedience, but it consists in His making easy for you the way of arriving at the everlasting and eternal kingdom [i.e. Paradise] through patience in setting desires aside for a few days [i.e. in this life]. This is the highest degree of generosity. Do not repeat to yourself the statements of those who are idle, but follow the men of resolution and prudence — the prophets and the righteous. Do not long to reap that which you did not sow. Would that all who fasted, performed ritual prayer, strove hard in the path of God, and kept all his duties, had been forgiven!

The sins [mentioned above] are all those against which you should guard the outward members of your body. The acts of these members certainly develop from the qualities of the soul (or mind). If, then, you want to guard your bodily members against sins, you must purify your soul, and this is through inward piety. The soul is that part of you, the soundness of which leads to the soundness of the whole body. [178] So be engaged in making it sound in order that your bodily members may be sound.

[175] Qur'ān 53:40.   [176] Qur'ān 52:16.
[177] Qur'ān 82:13f.
[178] Al-Bukhārī, *Ṣaḥīḥ*, Īmān, 39; Muslim, *Ṣaḥīḥ*, Musāqāt, 107; Ibn Māja, *Sunan*, Fitan, 14.

SINS OF THE SOUL

[A close connection exists between the body and the soul. The condition of the soul and the qualities it has acquired determine the nature of the acts of one's bodily members. [179] *The sins committed by these members, which were discussed in the preceding part of this book and against which every Muslim at the beginning of his guidance must guard himself, proceed from the sins of the soul, i.e. from the evil qualities of the soul. These qualities, therefore, must be removed. They are many in number. Three of them — envy, ostentation, and pride — which are commonly found in scholars, constitute the roots of all other evil qualities. So every Muslim at the beginning of his guidance must get rid of these three at least. In the following preamble and three sections, these are discussed — each of them is defined, its evil consequences are mentioned, and the methods of its removal from the soul are suggested.]*

[PREAMBLE]

Know that the vices of the soul are many, that the purification of the soul from vices is a lengthy task, and that the way of curing the soul of these vices is obscure. The knowledge and action of this cure have altogether disappeared because of people's inattention to themselves and their preoccupation with the vain pomp of this world. We have fully dealt with all this in our work, *The Revival of the Religious Sciences* — in its 'Quarter on Destructive Qualities of the Soul' and 'the Quarter on Saving Qualities'. But here we warn you against three evil qualities of the soul — which are predominant among the religious scholars of this time — so that you may be on your guard against these evil qualities, because these are both destructive in themselves and the roots of all other evil qualities of the soul. They are envy, ostentation and conceit. Strive after the purification of your soul from them. Should you be able to purify your soul from these, you will know how to guard against the remaining evil qualities discussed in 'the Quarter on the Destructive Qualities'. If you are unable to guard against these three, you will be more unable to guard against others.

Do not imagine that you will be able to preserve sound intention in your pursuit of knowledge while there is present any envy, ostentation or conceit in your mind. Indeed, the Prophet (may God bless him and greet him!) said,

---

[179] For a discussion of this see Muhammad Abul Quasem, "Psychology in Islamic Ethics", *Muslim World* (forthcoming).

"Three things are destructive. They are: avarice pursued unremittingly, desires given reign to, and having a high opinion of oneself." [180]

ENVY

Envy (*ḥasad*) stems from avarice: the miser is the one who is niggardly towards others with his possessions; the grudging person is the one who is niggardly towards the servants of God (exalted is He!) with God's favour which is in the treasury of His power and not in his own treasury — thus his avarice is stronger; the envious man is the one who is pained when God (exalted is He!) bestows from the treasuries of His power on one of His servants any favour in the form of knowledge, or wealth, or love for him in people's minds, or some piece of good fortune, and who therefore surely wants the removal of that favour from the other person, even though he himself will not obtain any advantage from its removal — this is the depth of evil, and it is for this reason [33] that the Messenger of God (may God bless him and greet him!) said,

"Envy eats up good deeds just as fire eats up wood." [181]

The envious man suffers punishment and is granted no mercy. He is continually suffering punishment in this world, because the world never lacks among his contemporaries and acquaintances many on whom God has bestowed His favour in the form of knowledge or wealth or influence; so he continually suffers punishment in this world until his death. 'The punishment of the Hereafter is severer and more lasting.' [182]

Indeed, a man does not arrive at the real faith (*īmān*) as long as he does not want for other Muslims what he wants for himself. [183] Indeed, he should be equal to them in weal and woe. The Muslims are like a single building, one part of which supports the other; [184] they are like a single body — if one member suffers, the rest of the body is affected. [185] Should you not find this condition present in

---

[180] Cf. Muslim, *Ṣaḥīḥ*, Birr, 56; Ibn Ḥanbal, *Musnad*, II, 160, 191, 195.

[181] Abū Dāwūd, *Sunan*, Adab, 44; Ibn Māja, *Sunan*, Zuhd, 22.

[182] Qur'ān 20:127. For a more detailed discussion of envy see al-Ghazālī, *Iḥyā'*, III. 182-200.

[183] Al-Bukhārī *Ṣaḥīḥ*, Īmān, 7; Muslim, *Ṣaḥīḥ*, Īmān, 71f.; at-Tirmidhī, *Sunan*, Qiyāma, 59; an-Nasā'ī, *Sunan*, Īmān, 19, 33; Ibn Māja, *Sunan*, Muqaddama, 9, Janā'iz, 1.

[184] Al-Bukhārī, *Ṣaḥīḥ*, Ṣalā, 88, Adab, 36, Maẓālim, 5; Muslim, *Ṣaḥīḥ*, Birr, 65; at-Tirmidhī, *Sunan*, Birr, 18; an-Nasā'ī, *Sunan*, Zakā, 67.

[185] Al-Bukhārī, *Ṣaḥīḥ*, Adab, 27; Muslim, *Ṣaḥīḥ*, Birr, 66.

your mind, then it is more important for you to be occupied with seeking deliverance from destruction than to be occupied with the less commonly required details of jurisprudence and the science of disputation with adversaries.

OSTENTATION

Ostentation (*riyā'*) is hidden polytheism (*ash-shirk al-khafī*), one of the two forms of polytheism. It consists in your seeking status in the minds of people so that you thereby obtain influence and respect. Love of influence is included in the "desires given reign to" [which are mentioned in a Tradition as destructive], and it is through this love that most people are destroyed. Yet people are destroyed only by themselves — if they really knew, they would realize that it is only their desire to show off which induced them to seek most of their knowledge and perform actions directed towards God (*'ibādāt*) not to mention their actions directed towards their fellow-men; this showing-off renders their acts of no avail, as is found in Tradition,

> "On the Day of Resurrection, orders will be given to take the martyr to Hell. He will entreat: Lord, I was martyred fighting in your path. God will retort: you wanted it to be said that so-and-so is brave, and that was already said, and that is your reward. The same will be said to the religious scholar, to the man who has performed the pilgrimage to Mecca, and to the reciter of the Qur'ān." [185a]

CONCEIT, PRIDE AND BOASTFULNESS

This is a chronic disease of the soul. It is man's consideration of himself as respectful and great and others as contemptible. The result of this mental quality in the case of the tongue is that he says, 'I am this, I am that', as accursed Iblīs said, 'I am better than he [i.e. Adam], for You have created me of fire and have created him of clay'. [186] The result [of a man's pride] in his association with people is his self-exaltation, self-advancement and seeking to be foremost in discussions, and his disdain for those who disagree with him. The proud man is he who, when he gives advice, mortifies, but, when he receives it, is rude. Everyone who considers himself better than any other of God's creatures (exalted is He!) [for whom he has contempt]

[185a] Cf. al-Bukhārī, *Ṣaḥīḥ*, Khumus, 10; Muslim, *Ṣaḥīḥ*, Imāra. 149; an-Nasa'ī, *Sunan*, Jihād, 21.

[186] Qur'ān 7:12.

is a proud man.

Indeed, you should know that the good man is he who is good in the estimation of God in the Home of the Hereafter; that, however is unknown to man, and is dependent upon the end to life (*al-khātima*). So your belief that you are better than others is sheer ignorance.

Indeed, you should not look at anyone except with the consideration that he is better than you and superior to you. Thus if you see a child, you should say, 'This person has not disobeyed God, but I have disobeyed; so he is undoubtedly better than I.' [34] If you see an older person, you should say, 'This man worshipped God before me, and so without any doubt he is better than I.' If the man whom you see is a learned man, you should say, 'This man has been given what I have not been given, has reached that stage which I did not reach, and has learnt that of which I am ignorant; so how can I be like him?' If the man whom you see is ignorant, you should say, 'This man has disobeyed God through ignorance, but I have disobeyed Him knowingly; so God's argument against me is stronger, and I do not know what end He will grant me and what end to him.' If the man you see is an infidel, you should say, 'I do not know perhaps he will accept Islam, his life will end in doing good, and because of acceptance of Islam he will be slipped out of his past sins [187] just as a hair is taken from dough gently; but as for me, perhaps God will cause me to go astray so that I become an infidel and my life will end in doing evil (I seek the protection of God from this). Consequently tomorrow [i.e. on the Day of Judgement) he will be among those drawn near to God and I shall be among those punished'.

Thus pride will leave your mind only when you know with certainty that the great man is he who is great in the estimation of God (exalted is He!); this [i.e. to be great in God's estimation] is dependent upon one's good state at the end to one's life concerning which there is doubt. Then the fear of the end will keep you from being proud at the expense of servants of God (exalted is He!), despite the existence of doubt concerning your fate. Your certain belief, your firm faith in God, at present does not exclude the possibility of change in the future, for God is the disposer of minds — He guides him whom He pleases and leads astray whom He pleases.

Prophetic traditions on envy, pride, ostentation, and conceit are numerous. The following single comprehensive Tradition will be

[187] Muslim, *Ṣaḥīḥ*, Īmān, 192.

sufficient for you concerning these [evil qualities of the mind].

Ibn al-Mubārak [188] related, with a chain of narrators going back to a certain man, that this man asked Mu'ādh: [189] O Mu'ādh. tell me a Tradition you heard from God's Messenger (may God bless him and greet him!). The man continued: Mu'ādh wept [at this question of mine] until I thought that he would not cease, but at length he ceased to weep; then he said: I heard God's Messenger (may God bless him and greet him!) saying to me,

"I am going to tell you a Tradition which is such that if you remember it, it will benefit you before God, but if you lose it and do not remember it, your plea of defence before God on the Day of Resurrection will be removed. O Mu'ādh, that Tradition is:

Verily God (blessed and exalted is He!), before creating the heavens and the earth, created seven angels, and appointed one of these seven angels as keeper of each of the seven heavens. Now the system is such that the guardian angels [190] ascend with man's deeds performed from morning to evening; each deed has a light like the light of the sun. After bringing it up to the lowest heaven they increase it and multiply it, and the keeper angel entrusted with this heaven says to the guardian angels, 'With this deed strike the face of its doer; I am in charge of backbiting; my Lord has commanded me not to allow a backbiter's deed to pass beyond me.'

Then the guardian angels bring one of man's good deeds and increase it and multiply it until they reach the second heaven with it. Then the keeper angel entrusted there says, 'Stop and with this deed strike the face of its doer, for through this deed he sought worldly honour; my Lord has commanded me not to allow his deed to pass beyond me, for he used to boast of his deed among his associates; [35] I am the angel in charge of boasting.'

---

[188] 'Abd Allāh ibn al-Mubārak (d. 181 A.H.), a Follower, was a noted ascetic, Traditionist, jurist, devotee, and philologist. See an-Nawawī, *Tahdhīb al-Asmā' wa l-Lughāt*, I, 285ff.

[189] Mu'ādh ibn Jabal (d. 18 A.H.), a famous companion of the Prophet, was one of the seventy Ansars who met him at 'Aqaba before the *hijra*. He took part in Badr, Uḥud, and all other battles in which the Prophet participated. He was one of the four

The guardian angels ascend with a man's deed — such as charity, ritual prayer, and fasting — which is so bright that it astonishes the guardians. They pass with it to the third heaven, and the angel responsible there says, 'Stop and with this deed strike the face of its doer; I am the angel in charge of pride; my Lord has commanded me not to allow his deed to pass beyond me, for he took pride at the expense of his associates.'

The guardian angels ascend with a man's deed — such as glorification of God, ritual prayer, fasting, the greater pilgrimage to Mecca (*hajj*), and the lesser pilgrimage to Mecca (*'umra*) — which is shining brightly like a star and resounding. When they pass with it to the fourth heaven, the angel in charge says, 'Stop and with this deed strike the face of its doer, his back, and his abdomen; I am in charge of conceit; my lord has commanded me not to allow his deed to pass beyond me, for whenever he did a deed he allowed conceit to enter into it.'

The guardian angels ascend with a man's deed until they pass with it to the fifth heaven. The deed is so embellished that it is like a bride being conducted to her husband. The angel entrusted with that heaven says, 'Stop and with this deed strike the face of its doer, carry it to him and place it on his shoulder; I am the angel in charge of envy; he used to envy whoever sought to acquire knowledge and performed a deed like his and all who were superior to men in some way; he used to envy them and slander them; my Lord has commanded me not to allow his deed to pass beyond me.'

The guardian angels ascend with a man's deed — such as ritual prayer, divine tax, the greater pilgrimage to Mecca, the lesser pilgrimage to Mecca, holy war, and fasting — which is as radiant as the moon. The angels pass with it to the sixth heaven. The angel in charge there says to them, 'Stop and with this deed strike the face of its doer, for he never showed mercy to anyone of God's servants who met with misfortune or disease, but felt pleasure in it; my Lord

from whom others should, the Prophet said, learn the Qur'ān. The Prophet also called him the most learned of all his companions in his grasp of matters lawful and unlawful. He was appointed by the Prophet the religious instructor and judge of the Yemen. He was a prolific narrator of Tradition. See Ibn al-Athīr, *Usd al-Ghāba*, IV, 376ff.; al-Munāwī, *Kawākib*, I, 71.   [190] Qur'ān 6:61, 82:1.

has commanded me not to allow his deed to pass beyond me.'

The guardian angels ascend with a man's deed — such as ritual prayer, fasting, spending of wealth in charity and in good causes, holy war, and piety — which has a sound like that of bees and a radiance like that of the sun and which was accompanied by three thousand angels. They pass with it to the seventh heaven. The angel entrusted with this heaven says to them, 'Stop and with this deed strike the face of its doer as well as his limbs, and lock up his mind; I veil from the Lord every action which is not intended for my Lord; by this deed he only sought something other than God (exalted is He!) — by it he certainly sought high rank among the learned men, mention among religious scholars, and reputation throughout the cities. My Lord has commanded me not to allow his deed to pass beyond me, for any action not performed purely for God is ostentation, and God does not accept the deeds of an ostentatious man.'

The guardian angels ascend with a man's deeds, such as ritual prayer, divine tax, fasting, the greater pilgrimage to Mecca, the lesser pilgrimage to Mecca, good character, observance of silence, [36] and remembrance of God (exalted is He!). Each deed is accompanied by the angels of the seven heavens until they have passed through all the veils to the presence of God (exalted is He!). They stand before Him, bearing witness to Him of the good deed done purely for God (exalted is He!). God (exalted is He!) says, 'You are the guardians over the deeds of My servant, but I am the watcher over his mind; he did not seek Me by this deed; he sought something other than Me; so on him is My curse: Then all the angels present say, 'Your curse and our curse be upon him!' The seven heavens and those who are there also curse him."

[Having heard this] Mu'ādh wept. He said: I asked, 'O Messenger of God, you are God's Messenger and I am Mu'ādh; how shall I have deliverance and salvation?' The Messenger of God retorted,

"Follow me even if there be some imperfection in your action. O Mu'ādh, guard your tongue against slandering your brothers, i.e. those who bear [i.e. believe in] the Qur'ān; ascribe your sins to yourself and not to them; do not ascribe purity to yourself and blame them; do not exalt yourself above them; do not mingle this-worldly activity with the activity of the Hereafter; do not be proud in your society so that men avoid you for your evil character; do not whisper to one man while another man is also present; do not magnify your importance over others so that the good things of this world and the Hereafter will depart from you; do not tear to pieces [the characters of] people with the result that on the Day of Resurrection the dogs of Hell will tear you to pieces in Hell. God (exalted is He!) said, 'By those who draw out violently ....' [191] Do you know what these are, O Mu'ādh?" I asked: What are they, O God's Messenger (may you be ransomed by my father and mother)? He replied, "They are the dogs in Hell drawing the flesh of its dwellers from their bones." I asked: O God's Messenger (may you be ransomed by my father and mother!), who is able to get rid of these evil qualities and who will escape from them? He replied, "Mu'ādh, it is indeed easy for him for whom God makes it easy."

Khālid ibn Mi'dān [192] said: I have not seen anyone more assiduous in reciting the great Qur'ān than Mu'ādh on account of this great Tradition.

Then, O you who desire knowledge, reflect on these evil qualities, i.e. pride ostentation and envy. Know that the greatest cause of the establishment of these defilements in the mind is the seeking of knowledge for the purpose of boasting and disputing with others. The common man is far removed from the most of these evil qualities, whereas the scholars are exposed to destruction because of them. Consider, then, which of your affairs is important — [a] to learn how to guard against these destructive qualities, to occupy yourself with the improvement of your mind and to prepare for your happiness in the Hereafter; [b] or to engage with others in seeking such knowledge as causes an increase in pride, ostentation, envy and conceit, so that you will perish along with those who perish.

Know that these three evil qualities of the mind, i.e. envy, pride, and ostentation, are from the root evil qualities of the soul. They have a single field of growth which is love of the world. It is for this

[191] Qur'ān 79:2.

[192] Khālid ibn Mi'dān (d. 103 or 104 A.H.),a Follower, was an ascetic, devotee, and gnostic who ascribed great value to intuitive knowledge. See al-Munāwī, *Kawākib*, I, 102.

reason that God's Messenger (may God bless him and greet him!) said,

"Love of this world is the fount of every sin." [193]

Despite this, this world is the seed-sowing field for the Hereafter. For him who takes from this world only that measure which is necessary, this world [37] is a seed-sowing field. [On the other hand,]   for him who wants this world in order that he may enjoy it, the world is the field of his destruction.

[CONCLUSION]

[*Al-Ghazālī here concludes the first and the second parts of this book and gives a logical reason for his passing on to the third part.*

All that is put in these two parts concerns the beginning of guidance, which is identical with the outward aspect of piety. After completing this aspect, one may study The Revival and practise the inward aspect of piety. On completion of this inward aspect, one will obtain knowledge through mystical intuition.

The beginning of guidance is in respect of man's dealings with God by performing His commands and avoiding His prohibitions. One who is at this stage of guidance associates with other people and also needs guidance for his association with them. Al-Ghazālī, therefore, feels it necessary to add a part dealing with this association. This is the logical transition to the third part of the book.] [194]

The above is a small part of the *outward* aspect of the science of piety, and it is the beginning of guidance . If you have tested your carnal soul in regard to the practice of it, and the soul has agreed with you upon this practice, then you must study *The Revival of the Religious Sciences* in order to learn the manner of reaching the *inward* aspect of piety. Then, when you have built up the interior of your mind in piety, at that state the veil between you and your Lord will be removed; the light of intuitive knowledge will be revealed to you, the springs of wisdom will burst forth from your mind, the secrets of the world of perception and the unseen world will be very clear to you so that you will hate these new-fangled sciences of which there was no mention in the days of the Companions (may God be

---

[193] This Tradition narrated by al-Bayhaqī and Ibn Abī d-Dunyā is often quoted by great ṣūfīs like al-Ghazālī (*Iḥyā'*, II, 202) and al-Makkī.

[194] Cf. Watt, "Authenticity", *JRAS*, 1952, pp. 24-45.

pleased with them!) and the Followers.

If, however, you seek knowledge from gossip, contradiction and dispute, then how great will be your misfortune, how prolonged your toil, how great your deprivation and loss! Do, then, whatever you like. This world which you seek by means of religion will not be vouchsafed to you, and the [happiness of the] Hereafter will also be kept from you. One who seeks this world by means of religion will lose both worlds, whereas one who forsakes this world for the sake of religion will gain both worlds.

The above is a short treatment of guidance at the beginning of the path of your dealings with God (exalted is He!) by performing what He commands and avoiding what He forbids.

Now I shall give you counsel by a short treatment of good manners so that you may charge your carnal soul with them in your association with servants of God (exalted is He!) and your companionship with them in this world.

PART THREE

ASSOCIATION WITH GOD AND MAN

[METHODS OF COMPANIONSHIP WITH GOD]

[God is everywhere and He sees and knows everything; He is always with man, although man does not see Him. In association with such an inseparable Companion, man has to take special consideration of Him. One who is practising the beginning of guidance should spend at least some of the day and night in complete devotion to God. At that time certain rules have to be observed, and these rules are set forth in this section.]

Know that your Companion who does not leave you, whether you are living in a place permanently or travelling, whether you are sleeping or awake, and indeed whether you are alive or dead, is He Who is your Lord, your Master, and your Creator. [195] Whenever you remember Him He is your Companion, as He (exalted is He!) said,

> "I am the Companion of him who remembers Me."

When your mind is filled with grief over your shortcomings in your religious duties, God is your inseparable Companion, as God (exalted is He!) said,

> "I am with those whose minds are filled with grief for My sake."

If you knew God truly and perfectly, you would take Him for a Companion and leave people aside. Should you be unable to do this all the time, take care that your day and night are not without a time in which you will be alone with your Master and enjoy the pleasure of your secret converse with Him. At that time you have to follow the

[195] Cf. Qur'ān 50:16, 57:4 — "He [i.e. God] is with you wherever you may be; He sees all that you do."

rules of companionship with Him (exalted is He!). So you must learn them.

The rules of companionship with God are: keeping silent with the head cast down, ignoring [one's surroundings], concentration of care and attention on God, continuance of silence, keeping the body's members at rest, hastening [38] to carry out His commands and avoiding His prohibitions, not complaining aganist fate, continual remembrance of God and reflection on Him, preference of the truth over falsehood, independence from people, humility before the awe of Him, brokenness of mind under the sense of shame, quiescence of mind from the worries of earning a livelihood while relying on the guarantee of sustenance given by God, [196] and trust in the bounty of God knowing that He chooses for man only that which is good for him.

All these should be your distinctive characteristics in all your days and nights, for they are the rules of companionship with a Companion Who does not leave you [at all], whereas [your companions from among] people sometimes leave you.

METHODS OF COMPANIONSHIP AND ASSOCIATION WITH PEOPLE

[A Muslim who is practising the beginning of guidance may, in his social life, come into the company of various groups of people, such as teachers, students, parents, friends, acquaintances, and common men who are not known to him. His behaviour with these groups of people should be like that of a good man, a pious man — behaviour which is demanded by humanity and which is prescribed by God and His Messenger. This kind of dealing will enable him to be successful in social life and to achieve happiness in the Hereafter. The rules governing such ideal Islamic behaviour are given in the following sections.]

[ASSOCIATION WITH STUDENTS]

If you are a learned man you should observe the rules of a man of knowledge which are seventeen in number: [1] patience, [2] continual forbearance, [3] sitting with awe in a dignified manner with the head cast down, [4] not to take pride at the expense of anyone except oppressors as a deterrent to their oppression, [5] preference

196 This refers to Qur'ān 11:6 — "There is no creature that moves in the earth but it is for God to provide it with sustenance, and He knows its temporary lodging and its permanent home. All this is recorded in a Clear Book [i.e. the Preserved Tablet]."

for humility in meetings and conferences, [6] not to jest and joke, [7] kindness towards students, [8] to act unhurriedly with the proud, [9] correction of the dull by suitable guidance without becoming enraged against them, [10] not to be too disdainful to confess one's own ignorance of a problem, [11] to give full attention to one who asks questions and to try to understand them, [12] acceptance of arguments of others, [13] to yield to the truth by turning towards it from error, [14] to forbid the student to acquire any such knowledge as is harmful to him, [15] to prevent him from intending to seek useful knowledge for anything other than the pleasure of God (exalted is He!), [16] to keep the student from occupying himself with 'collective obligation' before completing the 'individual obligation', [197] his 'individual obligation' being the correction of his outward (*ẓāhir*) and inward (*bāṭin*) self with piety (*taqwā*), and [17] the correction of himself with piety first so that his student may follow him first through his actions and then derive benefit from his words.

[ASSOCIATION WITH TEACHERS]

If you are a student you should observe the praiseworthy rules of a student's dealing with a learned man. These rules are: to greet the learned man first, to speak little in his presence, not to speak much so long as his teacher does not ask him anything, not to ask him questions before taking his permission, not to say, by way of objection to his words, 'So-and-so said contrary to what you have said', not to argue against his opinion in such a way as to show that he knows the truth more than his teacher, not to argue against his companions in his meeting, not to look around but to sit with downcast eyes, quietly and courteously as if he were engaged in a ritual prayer, not to speak to him much when he is tired, to stand up in order to show respect for him when he stands, not to follow him speaking and questioning and asking him questions along the street until he reaches home, not to imagine evil of him in regard to those of his actions which may appear abominable. The teacher knows better concerning his secret affairs.

When some actions of the teacher appear abominable, the student should recollect the complaint made by the prophet Moses to Khaḍir (may peace be on them both!), "Have you made a hole in the boat to drown the people in it? You have, indeed, done a strange thing!" [198] In fact Moses was wrong in his complaint which he made relying upon the outward appearance of what Khaḍir did.

197 See *supra*, n. 76.   198Qur'ān 18:71.

[ASSOCIATION WITH PARENTS]

If your parents are alive you should observe the rules of the behaviour of a child with his parents. These rules are: to listen to what the parents say, to stand up in order to show respect to them when they stand, to obey their orders, not to walk before them, not to raise [39] your voice over their voices, to answer to their call, earnestly to desire to please them, to be humbly tender with them, not to remind them of any good thing done for them or of any undertaking of their affairs, not to look at them askance, not to frown in their faces, [199] and not to travel [to a distant place] without their permission.

[COMPANIONSHIP WITH THE UNKNOWN COMMON MEN]

Know that people, besides teachers, students, and parents, are of three categories for you. They are either your friends, or those known to you but not intimately, or they are unknown to you. If you are involved with common men whom you do not know, you should observe the rules of sitting in company with common men.

The rules of companionship with common men are: avoidance of engagement in conversation with them, to listen very little to the news and rumours they spread, to feign unconcern with the bad words they habitually utter, to guard against meeting them frequently and against being in need of them, to warn them of their evil deeds with compassion, and to admonish them when there is hope that they may accept the admonition.

[ASSOCIATION WITH FRIENDS]

Concerning your brethren and friends, you have two tasks.

1. You should first consider the stipulations of companionship and friendship so that you will establish the relationship of brotherhood only with those who are fit for brotherhood and friendship. The Messenger of God (may God bless him and greet him!) said,

> "A man is considered by God to be of the religion of his intimate friend (*khalīl*); so let each of you consider whom he has taken for an intimate friend." [200]

When you try to find a companion in order that he may be your partner in the acquisition of knowledge and your companion in your

---

[199] Cf. Qur'ān 2:83, 180, 215, 4:36, 6:151, 17:23, 29:8, 31:14, 46:15, 17.
[200] At-Tirmidhī, *Sunan*, Zuhd, 45.

religious and secular matters, look for five qualities in him. [201]

The first quality is intelligence. There is no good in the companionship of a stupid man. Companionship with such a man ends in isolation and separation. The best of all that he will do to you is to harm you when he really intends to benefit you. An enemy who is intelligent is better than a friend who is stupid. Thus 'Alī [202] (may God be pleased with him!) said:

> Do not be in the company of an ignorant friend;
> Beware of him and let him beware of you.
>
> How often an ignorant man has brought destruction
> To a forbearing man who has befriended him.
>
> A man is likened with another man
> When that man walks with him.
>
> Like the similarity of one shoe to another
> When it is set opposite to it.
>
> A thing has patterns and resemblances from other things
> A soul reflects another soul which it encounters.

The second quality [of a prospective friend] is good character. Do not be the companion of a man whose character is bad. He is one who is unable to control himself when he is angry and is excited when he desires something. 'Alqama al-'Uṭāridī [203] (may God have mercy upon him!) gathered together the traits of good character in his will which he gave to his son at the time of his death. He said in that will,

> "Dear son, when you want the companionship of a man, be the companion of him who will preserve you when you employ him in your service, will adorn you if you are his companion, and will supply you with victuals when your victuals are not sufficient. Be the companion of him who

---

[201] Al-Makkī (*Qūt*, II, 442-89) and Miskawayh (*Tahdhīb*, pp. 160-66) discussed the qualities of a prospective friend, and their views influenced al-Ghazālī to a great extent. He thoroughly studied their works.

[202] 'Alī ibn Abī Ṭālib (d. 42 A.H.) was a cousin and son-in-law of the Prophet and the fourth rightly-guided caliph. His service to the cause of Islam both during and after the Prophet's lifetime was tremendous. For an account of him see Ibn Qutayba, *op. cit.*, pp. 203-18; Ibn 'Abd al-Barr, *al-Istī'āb*, III, 26-67.

[203] 'Alqama al-'Uṭāridī (d. 117 A.H.), a Follower, was a devotee of high order and ṣūfī. He was particularly conscious of traits of hypocrisy. See al-Munāwī, *Kawākib*, I, 82f.

will extend his helping hand to you when you extend to him
your hand for help, will reckon it a good thing if he sees
something good proceeding from you, but will stop an evil if
he sees it being done by you. Be the companion of a man
who will consider you truthful when you speak, will assist
you and help you if you desire anything and try for it, [40]
and will give you way if you both dispute on any matter."

'Alī (may God be pleased with him!) said reciting,

> Your true friend is he who is always with you,
> And he who harms himself in order to help you,
> And he who, when calamities of the time break you,
> Scatters his cloak in order to save you.

The third quality [of a prospective friend] is piety. Do not be the
companion of a wicked man (*fāsiq*) who persists in major sin. This is
because he who fears God does not persist in major sin, and he who
does not fear God may cause you mischief; indeed, his attitude
towards you will change with the changes in his luck and conditions.
God (exalted is He!) commanded his Prophet (may God bless him
and greet him!).

> "Do not follow him whose mind We have caused to be
> neglectful of remembrance of Us and who follows his
> passions, and whose case exceeds all bounds." [204]

Beware, then of associating with a wicked man, because the
constant sight of wickedness and sin will remove the dislike of sin
from your mind and will create the feeling that sin is something
light. The sinfulness of backbiting has become light to man's mind
for this reason and not for the reason that the mind cannot
understand it. If people see that a Muslim jurist is wearing a gold
ring or silkcloth, [205] they strongly oppose it because they rarely see
this, whereas they do not oppose backbiting even though it is a more
serious sin, because they always see this.

The fourth quality [of a prospective friend] is absence of greed.
Do not be the companion of a greedy man. Companionship of a man
greedy for the world is deadly poison, for human nature is such that
the nature of one man tends to resemble that of another and to

[204] Qur'ān 18:28.

[205] To wear a gold ring or silk cloth by a man, not by a woman, is forbidden in
Islam. See at-Tirmidhī, *Sunan*, Libās, 1; an-Nasa'ī, *Sunan*, Zīna, 40; Abū Dāwūd,
Sunan, Libās, 10; Ibn Māja, *Sunan*, Libās, 19.

imitate it; indeed, a man's nature steals the qualities of another man's nature in such a way that he is not aware of it. Therefore, association with a greedy man will increase your greed, and association with the ascetics will increase your asceticism.

The fifth quality [of a prospective friend] is truthfulness. Do not be the companion of a liar, for he is like the mirage: he will show that which is remote near to you and that which is near remote from you.

Perhaps these five qualities do not cease to exist in those who dwell in academic institutions and mosques [i.e. the intellectuals and the devotees]. You must do one of two things. Either you adopt solitude and loneliness, for in it lies your safety. Or you live in society, but your association with your fellow-men will be commensurate with their qualities. You must know that brotherhood is of three kinds — [1] a brother is for your good in the Hereafter, so that you will observe in him only the religious quality; [2] a brother is for your good in this world, so that you will observe in him only good character; and [3] a brother is a sociable companion, so that you must avoid his evil, disturbance and wickedness.

Men are of three categories. One is like food from which no one can be independent. Another is like medicine which is needed sometimes but not always. A third man is like a disease which is never needed but with which man is sometimes afflicted. This man is he in whom there is neither sociability nor benefit. Kind treatment of him is necessary so as to escape from him. In seeing him, there is a great benefit provided you are helped by God to obtain it. The benefit is that you perceive some of his wickedness and bad deeds and so you avoid them. Fortunate is he who is admonished by others; a believer in God (*al-mu'min*) is like a mirror of another believer. [206] Someone asked Jesus Christ (may peace be upon him!), "Who has taught you courtesy?" He replied, "None. Rather I saw the ignorance of the ignorant [41] and so avoided it." He (may God bless and greet him as well as our Prophet!) has indeed said the truth. If people were to avoid whatever they considered evil in others, they would possess perfect courtesy and need no one to instruct them in it.

[b] Your second task concerning your brethren and friends is to fulfil the duties of friendship and close companionship. When friendship is established and companionship between your friend and you exists, certain duties become incumbent upon you; the tie of

206 At Tirmidhī, *Sunan*, Birr, 18.

friendship makes them incumbent. In carrying out these duties, certain rules have to be followed. The Prophet (may God bless him and greet him!) said,

> "Two persons who have become brethren by the acceptance Islam are like two hands washing each other."

The Prophet (may God bless him and greet him!) once entered a thicket and picked up two tooth-sticks, one of which was crooked and the other straight. He gave the straight one to a certain companion of his who was with him and kept the crooked one for himself. His companion said, "Messenger of God, you deserve the straight one more than I." The Prophet (may God bless him and greet him!) replied,

> "Anyone who becomes the companion of another, even for only an hour of the day, will most certainly be asked [on the Day of Judgement] as to whether, in his companionship, he has fulfilled or neglected the duties set by God."

The Prophet (may God bless him and greet him!) further said,

> "Of two persons who keep company with each other, the more beloved to God (exalted is He!) is certainly he who is more kind to his companion."

The duties of friendship [207] are: 1. To help the friend financially even when one needs money for oneself. If this altruism is not possible, one should help the friend with one's surplus wealth at the time of his need. One should also assist him in his needs spontaneously, before he seeks assistance. 2. To hide his secrets, and to conceal his faults. 3. Not to convey to him others' disdain for him thereby making him unhappy . Rather to convey to him others' praise of him, thereby pleasing him. 4. To listen to him with full attention when he speaks and not to argue with him. 5. To call him with that name which he likes most, to praise him by mentioning his deeds that one knows, and to express gratitude to him in his presence for the good deeds he has done. 6. To defend the friend in his absence when aspersions are cast on his good repute, as one defends oneself. 7. To admonish him with kindness and in ambi-

[207] Ṣūfīs and Muslim philosophers alike emphasize the fulfilment of duties ot friendship. Ṣūfīs' emphasis, however, is stronger, and their treatment of these duties is more elaborate and closer to Islamic religious teachings on the subject. See al-Makkī, *Qūt*, II, 442-89; Miskawayh. *Tahdhīb*, pp. 160-66. Al-Ghazālī discussed these duties in great detail in *Iḥyā'*, II, 173-91.

guous terms when he needs admonition. 8. To forgive his faults and errors and not to blame him. 9. In one's solitude, to pray for the friend during his lifetime and also after his death. 10. To take care of a friend's wife and his other relatives after his death. 11. To choose to make things easy for the friend; so one will not charge him with the meeting of any of one's needs. 12. To give rest to his mind by removing causes of distress. 13. To express joy at all his delights, and to express sorrow at all unwanted things which happen to him, and to keep in mind that feeling for him which has been expressed to him so that one become truthful in one's friendship, both secretly and openly. 14. To greet the friend first when he approaches, to make room for him, to come out from the house to receive him, to see him off when he leaves, to keep silent when he speaks until he completes his conversation, and not to interrupt him when speaking.

In short, one is to behave with one's friend just as one would like him to behave with you. The brotherhood [i.e. friendship] of a man who does not want for his brother what he wants for himself [42] is hypocrisy (*nifāq*), and is an evil for him in this world and the Hereafter.

The above are the rules you have to follow when dealing with common men who are unknown to you and with friends taken as brothers.

[ASSOCIATION WITH ACQUAINTANCES]

Beware of your acquaintances, for you will receive only evil from those whom you do not know intimately. Your friends will render help to you, those who are completely unknown to you will not thwart you, but all evil will come upon you through those acquaintances who only express friendship with their tongues. So reduce the number of such acquaintances as far as possible.

When you are associated with acquaintances in an academic institution, or big mosque, or small mosque, or town, or market, you must not despise any one of them, for you do not know, perhaps he is better than you.

Do not consider them great in their worldly condition, lest you be destroyed; because the world has little worth in the estimation of God, and all that is in it is also of little value; so whenever worldly men appear to be great in your mind, you fall away from the eyes of God (exalted is He!). Guard yourself against using your religion in order to achieve some of their worldly possessions. Anyone who did this became insignificant in their eyes and was also deprived of their

105

possessions.

If your acquaintances are hostile to you do not face them with enmity, for you are unable to be patient when they requite you; so your religious nature will disappear in their enmity towards you; thus your difficulties with them will be prolonged. [On the other hand], if they respect you, praise you in your presence and express their friendship for you, do not trust them, for if you enquire into the real nature of this you will not find even one per cent of them sincere in their behaviour. Do not expect that their behaviour will be the one and the same in public and in private. Do not be astonished if they rebuke you in your absence and do not be angry for that, because, should you be fair, you would find similar behaviour in yourself even concerning your friends and relatives, and indeed concerning your teachers and parents — in their absence you talk of things concerning them which you will not mention in their presence.

Completely abandon your greed for wealth, influence and assistance from your acquaintances. A greedy man usually becomes loser in the future and is necessarily humiliated at the present time. If you ask anyone of them to satisfy your needs and he does so, be grateful to God as well as to him; if, however, he falls short, do not blame him and do not complain against him [to anyone], lest enmity arise between him and you. Be like a believer in God (*al-mu'min*) who seeks to find excuses for people, and do not be like a hypocrite who seeks to find fault; say, 'Perhaps the man fell short of satisfying my need for a reason which I do not know.'

Do not suppose that any of your acquaintances will accept your opinion unless you first perceive an indication of his acceptance; otherwise he will not listen to you but will be your adversary. When one of them has made a mistake and is abstaining from teaching of anyone, do not teach him because he will be benefited by learning from you and [at the same time] will be your enemy. If, however, his mistake has led him to the commission of a sin, tell them the truth with kindness, not with roughness.

When you see that they respect you and do good to you, be grateful to God Who has made you beloved to them. But if you find them doing evil to you, entrust them to God [43], seek the protection of Him (exalted is He!) against their evil, do not reproach them, and do not say, 'Why do you not recognize my right seeing that I am so-and-so, the son of so-and-so, and seeing that I am a learned man?' Do not say this because it is the stupid men who say this. The most stupid man is he who ascribes purity to himself and praises himself. Know that God gives them power over you [so that they do evil to you] only for sins you have committed. So seek forgiveness of God for your sins. Know also that God's placing them in power over you is His punishment of you.

Be such among your acquaintances that you hear their truth but are blind to their falsehood, speak of their good qualities but keep silent about their evil qualities.

Beware of association with the learned men of this time, [208] especially those occupied with controversial problems and intellectual disputes. Beware of them; because of their jealousy 'they wait for you to fall into ill-fortune, [209] imagine various things concerning you, and behind your back make signs with their eyes among themselves while enumerating your faults when they meet together so that sometimes in their anger they confront you with these faults during their rivalries. They do not forgive your faults or slips; nor do they hide your private matters which should be kept hidden. They make an account with you even in the most negligible matter, and they envy you in everything, small or great. They instigate your friends against you by slandering, spreading false information, and lies. If they are pleased with you they show it through servile flattery; if they are angry with you they are quietly stupid. On their bodies they wear beautiful clothes, but their minds are wolves. This is a judgement based on clear observation of most of them except those whom God (exalted is He!) has protected. Companionship with them is a loss, and association with them is to be forsaken by them.

If the above is the judgement on those who express their friendship to you, how grave will be the judgement on those who openly declared their enmity towards you? Al-Qāḍī ibn Maʿrūf (may God bestow mercy upon him!) said:

> Beware of your enemy once,
> But beware of your friend a thousand times,
> For a friend turns to be an enemy sometimes,
> And then knows better how to harm you.

In the same vein a certain poet said:

> Your enemy sometimes comes from your friend,
> So do not increase the number of friends;
> Most of the diseases that you see,
> Originate from eating and drinking.

[208] See *supra*, n. 152. [209] Qurʾān 52:30.

Be as Ḥilāl ibn al-'Alā' [210]   aid:

> When I forgave and bore no rancour to anyone,
> I gave rest to myself from anxiety about enemies.

> I greet my enemy when I see him,
> That I may repel evil by greetings.

> I express cheerfulness to a man I hate,
> As if he has filled my mind with delights. [44]

> I am not safe from those whom I do not know,
> So how can I be safe from those who are friends?

> Men are a disease and the only remedy is forsaking them,
> By being harsh with them we cut off brotherhood.

> Then keep men at a safe distance and you will be safe from
>   their mischiefs,
> And be earnestly desirous of requiring friendship.

> And behave well with men and endure what comes from
>   them;
> Be deaf, dumb, blind and one who is God-fearing.

Also, as a certain wise manadmonished, "Meet your friend and your enemy with a pleasing countenance, without lowering oneself and without fear of them; and be dignified without pride, be humble without lowering oneself." In all your affairs be moderate; extremes in all affairs are blameworthy, as a certain poet said:

> You must be moderate in all affairs,
> For this is a straight path to the plain road;
> Do not be excessive or deficient concerning anything,
> For both states of affairs are blameworthy.

Do not look in pride to the left and to the right and do not look around much. Do not stand beside a group of men, but sit with them; and when you sit, do not sit so as to be ready to rise. Be on your guard against fiddling with your fingers, playing with your beard and your rings, picking the teeth, inserting your fingers into your nostrils, spitting a lot, blowing or wiping your nose, driving flies away from your face, spreading the arms about while walking, yawning in the faces of people, and during ritual prayers   and so on.

[210] Hilal ibn al-'Alā' (d.154 A.H.) was a poet and Qur'ān-reader (*qārī*). See Ibn Qutayba, *al-Ma'ārif*, ed. Tharwat 'Ukāsha, Cairo, 1969, pp.531, 540.

Let your meetings be a guide to the truth and your talk be orderly and arranged. Listen to good talk from those who speak to you, without expressing excessive surprise, and do not ask them to repeat it. Be silent in the case of things which make one laugh and stories. Do not speak of your high opinion of your child, poetry, speech, books, and all other things which are special to you. Do not take on affectations like an adorned woman. Do not adopt a style like the style of a slave. Guard against the use of too much collyrium and oil, and do not ask too much for help in your needs.

Do not encourage anyone to injustice and oppression. Do not make the amount of your wealth known to your wife or child let alone others, for if they find it small they will have contempt for you, and if they find it enormous you will never be able to please them with wealth. Be strict with them without treating them harshly, and be tender with them without weakness. Do not jest with female servants or male servants, lest your dignity fall. When you dispute, be patient, protect yourself from your ignorance and haste, and think of your proof. Do not hint a lot with your hands. Do not look often behind you. Do not kneel on your knees. Speak when your anger is appeased. When the ruler brings you near to him, be on the edge of the spear-head.

Beware of one who is your friend only when you are healthy and prosperous, for he is the greatest of [45] all your enemies. Do not make your wealth more valuable than your honour.

This treatment, O young man, is sufficient for you concerning the beginning of guidance. Test yourself with it. It consists of three parts. One on the rules of acts of devotion to God, one on the avoidance of sins, and one on the association with people. This association includes all dealings of a man with the Creator and the creatures. Should you find this beginning of guidance suitable to you and your mind inclined to it and desirous of acting in accordance with it, then know that you are a man whose soul God has illuminated and broadened with faith (*īmān*). Be confirmed that this beginning of guidance has an end and that beyond it exist secrets, depths, wider knowledge, and visions and intuitions (*mukāshafāt*). These we have set forth in our work, *The Revival of the Religious Sciences*. Be occupied then with the attainment of it. If you find that your carnal soul does little in accordance with these duties (*wazā'if*) and sets aside this type of knowledge and says to you, 'How can this knowledge benefit you in the meetings of the scholars?, when will it put you in the forefront among your peers and men of reflection?, and how can it elevate your status in the assembly of princes and governors in order that it may bring you to wealth and other means of living, to the management of endowments and to the post of a judge and magistrate?,' then realize that Satan has misled you and has caused you to forget the place to which you will return and the place of dwelling after death. So seek for yourself a Satan like yourself in order that he may teach you that knowledge which, you imagine, will benefit you and bring you to what you desire. But then know that the kingdom will never be pure for you in your locality, let alone your village and town; then, on the Day of Judgement, you will miss the eternal kingdom and the everlasting delight in the near presence of the Lord of all the worlds.

May peace, God's mercy and blessings be upon you! Praise be to God first and last, outwardly and inwardly! There is no ability or power except with God, the High, the Great. May God bless and greet our leader, Muḥammad, and his family and his companions! [46].

BIBLIOGRAPHY

'Abd ar-Razzāq. *Iṣṭilāḥāt aṣ-Ṣūfiyya.* Edited by Aloys Sprenger, Calcutta, India, 1845.

Abel, Almond. "Dadjdjāl." *EI* [2], II, 76-77.

Abū Dāwūd, Sulaymān ibn al-Ash'ath as-Sijistānī. *Sunan.* 2 vols. Cairo, 1935.

Abul Quasem, Muhammad. *The Ethics of al-Ghazālī: a Composite Ethics in Islam.* 2nd ed. New York, 1978.

—. *The Jewels of the Qur'ān: al-Ghazālī's Theory.* Kuala Lumpur, 1977.

—. *The Recitation and Interpretation of the Qur'ān: al-Ghazālī's Theory.* Kuala Lumpur, 1979.

—. *Salvation of the Soul and Islamic Devotions.* Kuala Lumpur, 1979.

—. "Al-Ghazālī's Conception of Happiness." *Arabica*, XXII (1975), 153-61.

—. "Al-Ghazālī's Rejection of Philosophic Ethics." *IS*, XII, No. 2 (1974), 111-27.

—. "Al-Ghazālī's Theory of Devotional Acts." *IQ*, XVIII, 48-61.

—. "Al-Ghazālī's Theory of Good Character." *IC*,(1978), pp.229-39.

Afnan, Soheil. *Philosophical Terminology in Arabic and Persian.* Leiden, 1964.

'Allām, Muḥammad Mahdī. "Al-ḥasad 'ind al-Ghazālī." *Abū Ḥāmid al-Ghazālī fī adh-Dhikrā al-Mi'awiyya at-Tāsi'a li-Milādihi.* Edited by Zakī Najīb Maḥmūd. Cairo, 1961, pp. 219-37.

Arberry, A.J. *Ṣūfism: An Account of the Mystics of Islam.* London, 1950.

Al-'Asqalānī, Ibn Ḥajar. *Tahdhīb at-Tahdhīb.* 12 in 6 vols. Hyderabad, India, 1325-27 A.H.

   Al-Iṣāba fī Tamyiz aṣ-Ṣaḥāba. 4 vols. Egypt, 1358/1939.

'Aṭṭār, Farīd ad-Dīn. *Tadhkirat al-Awliyā'.* Edited by R.A. Nicholson, London and Leyden, 1907.

Al-Bayḍāwī, 'Abd Allāh. *Anwār at-Tanzīl wa Asrār at-Ta'wīl.*

Egypt, 1923.

Blashdell, R.A. "Religious Values in al-Ghazālī's Works" *MW*, XXXVI (1946), 115-20.

Boer, Tjilze de, and Gardet L. "Ālam," *EI*,²I, 349-52.

Buhl, Frants. "Subḥān Allāh." *EI*, IV, 492-93.

Al-Bukhārī, Muḥammad bin Ismā'il. *Ṣaḥīḥ*. 9 vols. Egypt, 1377 A.H.

Coulson, Noel J. *Conflict and Tensions in Islamic Jurisprudence*. Chicago, 1969.

Adh-Dhahabī, Abū 'Abd Allāh Muḥammad. *Tadhkirat al-Ḥuffāẓ*. 4 vols. Hyderabad, India, 1333-34 A.H.

—. *Mīzān al-I'tidāl fī naqd ar-Rijāl*. 4 vols. Cairo, 1963.

Al-Fīrūzabādī, Abū Ṭāhir Muḥammad ibn Ya'qūb. *Al-Qāmūs al-Muḥīṭ*. 4 vols. 3rd ed. Cairo, 1344/1925.

Gabrieli, F. "Adab." *EI*,²I, 175-76.

Gardet, L. "Un probleme de mystique comparee: La mention du nom divin (*dhikr*) dans la mystique musulmane." *RT*, LII (1952), 642-79; LIII (1953), 197-216.

—. "Dhikr." *EI*², II, 223-27.

—. "Du'ā'." *EI*², II, 617-18.

Al-Ghazālī, Abū Ḥāmid Muḥammad, *Al-Arba'īn fī Uṣūl ad-Dīn*. Egypt, 1344 A.H.

—. Ayyuhā l-Walad. Translated into English by George H. Scherer, Beirut, 1933.

—. *Bidāyat al-Hidāya*. Egypt, n.d.

—. *Iḥyā' 'Ulūm ad-Dīn*. 5 vols. Beirut, n.d.

—. *Al-Iqtiṣād fī l-I'tiqād*. Cairo, 1320 A.H.

—. *Jawāhir al-Qur'ān*. 2nd ed. Cairo, 1933.

—. *Kīmiyā'-i-Sa'ādat*. Tehran, 1319 A.H.

—. *Al-Maqṣad al-Asnā Sharḥ Asmā' Allāh al-Ḥusnā*. Egypt, n.d.

—. *Mishkāt al-Anwār*. Translated into English by W.H.T. Cairdner. London, 1924.

—. *Al-Munqidh min aḍ-Ḍalāl*. Translated into English by W. Montogmery Watt. London, 1953.

—. *Al-Qisṭās al-Mustaqīm*. Edited by al-Yasu'i. Beirut, 1959.

—. *Tahāfut al-Falāsifa*. Edited by Sulaymān Dunyā. Cairo, n.d.

—. *Al-Wajīz*. Cairo, 1317 A.H.

Goitein, Solomon D.F. "The Origin and Nature of the Muslim Friday Worship." *MW*, XLIX (1959), 183-95.

Goldziher, Ignaz. "Bismillāh." *ERE*, II, 666-68.

Hass, William S. "The Zikr of the Rahmanija-Order in Algeria: A

Psycho-Physiological Analysis." *MW*, XXXIII (1943), 16-28.

Hourani, George F. "The Chronology of Ghazālī's Writings." *JAOS*, LXXIX (1959), 225-33.

Hughes, Thomas Patrick. *Dictionary Of Islam*. London, 1885.

Al-Hujwīrī, 'Alī Ibn 'Uthmān. *Kashf al-Maḥjūb*. Translated into English by R.A. Nicholson. Leyden, 1911.

Ibn 'Abd al-Barr. *Al-Istī'āb*. 4 vols. Egypt, 1960.

Ibn al-Athīr. *Usd al-Ghāba*. 5 vols. Egypt, 1280 A.H.

Ibn al-Ḥajjāj, Muslim. *Ṣaḥīḥ*. 16 vols. Cairo, 1929.

Ibn Ḥanbal, Aḥmad. *Musnad*. 6 vols. Cairo, n.d.

Ibn Hishām. *As-Sīrat an-Nabawiyya*. 2 vols. Edited by Muṣṭafā as-Saqā *et al.* 2nd ed. Egypt, 1955/1375.

Ibn Khallikān, Abū l-'Abbās. *Wafayāt al-A'yān wa Anbā' Abnā' az-Zamān*. Cairo, 1299 A.H.

Ibn Māja, Muḥammad ibn Yazīd al-Qazwīnī. *Sunan*. 2 vols. Edited by Muḥammad Fu'ād 'Abd al-Bāqī. Cairo, 1952-53.

Ibn Manzūr, Jamāl ad-Dīn Muḥammad ibn Mukarram al-Anṣārī. *Lisān al-'Arab*. 20 vols. Cairo, 1308/1901.

Ibn an-Nadīm, Muḥammad. *Al-Fihrist*. Edited and translated into English by Bayard Dodge. 2 vols. New York & London, 1970.

Ibn Qutayba. *Al-Ma'ārif*. Edited by Thrwat 'Ukāsha. Cairo, 1969.

Ibn Taymiyya, Taqī ad-Dīn. *At-Tawassul wa l-Wasīla*. Beirut, 1390/1970.

Al-Isfahānī, Abū l-Qāsim ar-Rāghib. *Adh-Dharī'a ilā Makārim ash-Sharī'a*. Cairo, 1299/1882.

Al-Isfahānī, Abū Nu'Aym. *Ḥilyat al-Awliyā' wa Ṭabaqāt al-Aṣfiyā'*. 10 vols. 2nd ed. Beirut, 1387/1969.

Al-Jurjānī, Abū l-Ḥasan al-Ḥusayn. *At-Ta'rīfāt*. edited by G. Flügel. Leipzig, 1845.

Al-Kalābādhī, Abū Bakr Muḥammad. *At-Ta'arruf li-Madhhab Ahl at-Taṣawwuf*. Edited by 'Abd al-Ḥalīm Maḥmūd and Ṭāha 'Abd al-Bāqī Surūr. Cairo, 1380/1960.

Krenkow, Fritz. "Sadj'." *EI*, IV, 43-44.

Lane, E.W. *An Arabic-English Lexicon*. Edited by Stanley Lan-Poole. 8 vols. London. 1863-93.

Lazaruth-Yafeh, H. "Place of the Religious Commandments in the Philosophy of al-Ghazālī." *MW*, LI (1961), 173-84.

Macdonald, D.B. *Development of Religious Attitude and Life in Islam*. Beyrut, 1965.

—. "Ḥamdala" *EI²*, III, 122-23.

Al-Makkī, Abū Ṭalīb. *Qūt al-Qulūb*. 2 vols. Cairo, 1961/1381.

Miskawayh, Abū 'Alī Aḥmad. *Tahdhīb al-Akhlāq*. Edited by Constantine K. Zurayk. Beirut, 1968.

Al-Munāwī, 'Abd ar-Ra'ūf. *Al-Kawākib ad-Durriyya*. Edited by Maḥmūd Ḥasan Rabī'. 2 vols. Cairo, 1938/1357.

Nakamura, Kojiro. *Ghazālī on Prayer*. Tokyo, 1973.

An-Nasā'ī, Abū 'Abd ar-Raḥmān ibn Shu'ayb. *Sunan*, 8 vols. Egypt, 1383-84/1964-65.

An-Nawawī. *Tahdhīb al-Asmā' wa l-Lughāt*. 4 vols. Egypt, n.d.

Nicholson, R.A. *Studies in Islamic Mysticism*. Cambridge, England, 1921.

—. "Badal." *SEI*, p. 55.

Padwick, Constance E. *Muslim Devotions*. London, 1961.

Pedersen, Johannes. "Masdjid" *SEI*, pp. 330-33.

Al-Qushayrī, Abū l-Qāsim. *Ar-Risāla*. 2 vols. Edited by 'Abd al-Ḥalīm Maḥmūd and Maḥmūd ibn ash-Sharīf Cairo, 1966/1385.

Riḍā, M. *Abū Ḥāmid al-Ghazālī*. Cairo, 1924.

Robson, J. "Ḥadīth Kudsī." *EI*[2], III, 28-29.

As-Sarrāj, Abū Naṣr. *Kitāb al-Luma'*. Edited by R.A. Nicholson. London, 1963.

Schimmel, Annemarie. "Some Aspects of Mystical Prayer in Islam." *DWT*, N.S.II (1952), 112-25.

Ash-Shāfi'ī, Imām. *Ar-Risāla fī Uṣūl al-Fiqh*. Translated into English by Majid Khadduri. Baltimore, 1961.

Ash-Sha'rānī. *At-Ṭabaqāt al-Kubrā*. 2 in 1 vol. Cairo, 1373/1954.

Ash-Shurunbalālī, ibn 'Ammār. *Matn Nūr al-Īḍāḥ*. Cairo, 1389/ 1969.

Smith, Margaret. *Rābi'a: the Mystic and Her Fellow Saints in Islam*. Cambridge, England, 1928.

— "Al-Ghazālī on the Practice of the Presence of God." *MW*, XXIII (1933), 16-23.

As-Sulamī, *Ṭabaqāt aṣ-Ṣūfiyya al-Kubrā*. Edited by Nūr ad-Dīn. Egypt, 1953/1372.

At-Tahānawī, Muḥammad A'lā ibn 'Alī. *Kashshāf Iṣṭilāḥāt al-Funūn*. Edited by Aloys Sprenger and W Nassau Less. 5 vols. Beirut, 1966.

At-Tirmidhī, Abū 'Īsā Muḥammad, *Sunan*. 13 vols. Egypt, 1931- 34.

Watt, W. Montgomery. *Muslim Intellectual: a Study of al-Ghazālī*. Edinburgh, 1963.

— "The Authenticity of the Works Attributed to al-Ghazālī."

JRAS, 1952, pp. 24-45.

Wensinck, A.J. *The Muslim Creed*. Cambridge, England, 1932.

— "Ka'ba." *SEI*, pp. 191-98.

— "Shafā'a." *SEI*, pp. 511-12.

— "Malā'ika." *SEI*, pp. 318-20.

— "Takbīr." *EI*, IV, 627.

Al-Yāfi'ī. *Mir'āt al-Janān wa 'Ibrat al-Yaqẓān*. 4 in 2 vols. Hyderabad, India, 1337-38.

Az-Zabīdī, as-Sayyid al-Murtaḍā. *Itḥaf as-Sādat al-Muttaqīn bi-Sharḥ Asrār Iḥyā' 'Ulūm ad-Dīn*. 10 vols. Cairo. 1311 A.H.

Az-Zamakhsharī, Abū l-Qāsim Jār Allāh. *Al-Kashshāf an Ḥaqā'iq at-Tanzīl*. 4 vols. Egypt, 1385/1966.

Zewemer, S.M. *Studies in Popular Islam*. London, 1939.

— "Animistic Elements in Moslem Prayer." *MW*, VIII (1918), 359-75.

Al-Qur'ān al-Karīm (bi-r-rasm al-'Uthmanī) Edited in Egypt, n.d.

(The meaning of abbreviations used in this bibliography is given on p. 16)

INDEX

(The Arabic article *al-*, with its variants such as *an, ash, ad, at, as,* is disregarded in the alphabetical arrangement. The articles 'the', 'a' and 'an' before English language titles are also not taken into consideration.)

GENERAL INDEX

al-Bukhārī, 23, 26ff., 30, 35, 38, 45, 47, 58, 63, 65-68, 70-73, 75f., 80, 86, 88f.

caliph, 101
character, 76, 93f., 101, 103
charity, 92f.
child, children, 51, 90, 100, 109
commands of God, 11, 18, 22-25, 45, 85, 91f., 95f., 98
companion of Prophet, 18, 28, 36, 44, 77, 91, 95, 104, 110; greatest of, 81; most learned of, 92
companionship, association: with God, 13, 97f.; with people, 11, 13, 24, 49, 63, 89, 95-110.
conceit, 87, 89-95
consensus of Muslim community, 76
contempt, contemptible, 74, 89, 109
Contrites' Ritual Prayer, 52
cursing, 74f., 79f., 93

Dajjāl, 21
ad-Dārimī, 20, 70
da'wāt, 42
Dawn Prayer, 11, 27, 35-38, 40, 42, 44f., 49, 54, 59f., 63f.
Day of Judgement, Day of Resurrection, Day of Doom, Day of Eternity, 9, 20, 29-32, 37f., 54, 73, 78, 80, 84, 89ff., 94, 104, 110
death, 20, 22, 24, 43, 49, 54-57, 85, 101, 105, 110
demonic, see Satan
desire, carnal, 72, 82
devotee, 47, 62, 91, 94, 103
devout, most, 72, 81
dhikr, 38
Dhū l-Hijja, 68f.
Dhū l-Qa'da, 69
disciple, see student
dispute, 74, 78f., 89, 94, 96, 107, 109
distance from God, 20
Doomsday, see Day of Resurrection

East, 10
Egyptian, 14
EI, 115.
EI,[2] 40
end of life, 20, 90

enemy, enmity, 30, 38, 42, 58, 101, 106-109
English, 62
envy, envious, 12, 87ff., 90. 92, 94, 107
The Ethics of al-Ghazālī ..., 11, 18, 42, 48, 51, 58
Evening Prayer, 11, 52, 60, 63
evil, invoking of, 74f., 80

falsehood, 76, 98, 107
family, 13, 47, 51, 58; of Prophet, 18, 36, 40, 44, 110
al-Fārābī, 10
farḍ al-'ayn, 46
fāsiq, 102
fasting, 12, 29, 49, 57, 65, 68-71, 76, 86, 92f.; aim and significance of, 12, 68, 70
fate, 98
father, 25, 94
Fāṭima, 41
Fayṣal at-Tafriqa..., 79
fear of God, 35, 45, 67, 102
fighter, fighting, 72, 89
flattery, 107
flight, 72
Follower, 9, 62, 91, 94, 96, 101
Forenoon Prayer, 45
forgiveness of God, 14, 19, 26, 32, 35f., 43f., 50f., 54f., 58, 61, 65, 85f., 107; of man, 105, 108
Friday: as best day, 12, 65
Friday Assembly Prayer, 12, 57, 65-68
friend, friendship, 13, 34, 42, 51, 98, 100-109; qualities of, 101ff.; duties of, 103ff.
funeral, 47

Al-Ghazālī, Abū Ḥāmid, 10-14, 18, 20, 49, 51, 54, 58, 62, 65, 68, 76f., 79ff., 83, 88, 95, 101, 104
ghusl, 33
glorification: of self, 74f., 77ff., 89; of God, 32, 36, 38, 40, 42ff., 47, 51, 59ff., 63ff., 70
gnostic, 94
God, divine, King, Master, 9-110 passim; remembrance of, 24, 29, 32f., 56, 93, 98, 102; near to, 12, 20, 23, 33, 48,

Ṣalāt al-'Aṣr, 50
Ṣalāt al-Awwābīn, 52
Ṣalāt aḍ-Ḍuḥā, 45
Ṣalāt al-Fajr, 35
Ṣalāt al-'Ishā', 52
Ṣalāt al-Jamā'a, 62
Ṣalāt al-Jumu'a, 65
Ṣalāt aẓ-Ẓuhur, 49
Ṣalāt al-Witr, 53
salutation in ritual prayer, 39, 64
salvation, 13, 23, 49, 93
Salvation of the soul..., 62
Satan, demon, 10, 13, 19ff., 26ff., 32, 45ff., 53, 57, 59, 61, 63, 67, 78, 82
Saturday, 65
scholar, religious, 10, 18, 21, 45, 79, 87, 89, 93f., 109
seclusion, solitude, 24, 49, 81, 103, 105
secular, 75, 78, 101
self-examination, 58
self: outward, 12, 23, 99; inward, 12, 23, 99
sex, sexual, 12, 23, 33, 68ff., 83, 99
Sha'bān, 69
Sharī'a, 10, 65
Shī'a, 10
ash-shirk al-khafī, 89
sick, 47, 56
siesta, 49
sincerity, 40
Sincerity, Statement of, 25, 29
sinner, sin: of body, 11ff., 19, 21, 24, 32, 35f., 42, 46ff., 54f., 65, 69, 72-87, 90, 95, 102, 109; of ear, 12, 73f.; of eyes, 12, 73f.; of feet, 12, 73, 84; of genitals, 12, 73, 83; of hands, 12, 73, 83f.; of stomach, 12, 73, 81ff.; of tongue, 12, 73-81; of soul, mind, 12f., 86-95, 109
slandering, 69, 92f., 107
slave, 24, 44, 83, 109
sleep, 11, 49; good manners of, 54-57; waking from, 11f., 24f.
sociable, 103
social, society, 13, 46, 98, 103
soul, mind, 11ff., 18, 23f., 33, 35-109 *passim;* carnal, 13, 19, 22, 46, 56, 58, 95-98, 109; *see also* body
story-teller, 67
student, disciple, 13f., 98ff.

submissiveness, 57f., 62, 67
ṣūfī, ṣūfīsm, mystical, 10, 45, 47f., 62, 82, 95, 101, 104
sūfīsm, *see* ṣūfī
sū' al-khātima, 20
Sunan: of Abū Dāwūd, 9f., 19f., 30, 47, 53, 62, 67, 72f., 75, 78, 80, 88, 102; of ad-Dārimī, 20; of Ibn Māja, 19ff., 26, 69f., 72, 85f., 88, 102; of an-Nasā'ī, 19f., 30, 47, 62, 66f., 70, 72, 76, 88f., 102; of at-Tirmidhī, 19f., 26f., 30, 45, 47, 50, 53, 65, 67, 70, 73, 76, 78, 80, 85, 88, 100, 102f.
sunna, 35ff., 45, 52f., 66f.; emphasized, 34, 50; fixed, 52; *mu'akkada,* 34
sunnī, 10
sun-rise, 11, 36, 42ff., 51
Sunset Prayer, 11, 51f., 60, 63, 67
supererogatory, 23, 34ff., 44, 47ff., 52ff., 67f.
supplication to God, 20, 24-30, 32f., 35-40, 42, 51f., 55, 61-64, 67f,
sustenance, 98

aṭ-ṭā'at, 72
at-Ṭabarī, ibn Jarīr, 65
tābi'ī, 62
aṭ-Ṭabrānī, 74
Tahajjud Prayer, 49
Tahdhīb al-Akhlāq, 101f., 104
Tahdhīb al-Asmā' ..., 91
Tahdhīb at-Tahdhīb, 81
taḥiyyat al-masjid, 49, 66
taqwā, 18, 99
Tārīkh al-Umam..., 65
tasbīḥ, tasbīḥāt, 38, 42
tashahhud, 61
at-Tawassul wa l-Wasīla, 39
tax, divine (*zakā*), 12, 71, 92f.
tayammum, 34f.
teacher, 13f., 18, 85, 98ff., 106
theologian, theological, 9, 46, 62, 78f.
Thursday, 65
at-Tirmidhī, 19f., 26., 30, 45, 47, 50, 53, 65, 67, 70, 73, 76, 78, 80, 85, 88, 100, 102f.
tooth-stick, 27f., 54, 65, 104
Tradition (*ḥadīth*) 9, 10, 13, 19, 27f., 33, 40, 44f., 47, 50, 52f., 63f. 66-69, 74ff.,

INDEX OF QUR'ĀNIC SŪRAS AND VERSES CITED

a) Index of Qur'ānic Sūras Cited

b) Index of Qur'ānic Verses Cited